THE ADVENTURE OF FAITH

A Journey into the Heart of God

JAMES SMITH

©2023
The Adventure of Faith - by James Smith

Cover Design by Carolyn Smith
Layout by Tom Carroll
Edited by Katherine Vlaanderen

ISBN: 978-0-6459271-0-8

All rights reserved. No part of this publication may be reproduced, stored in a retrieval system, or transmitted in any form or by any means – for example, electronic, photocopy, recording - without the prior written permission of the publisher. The only exception is brief quotation in printed reviews.

All scripture quotations, unless otherwise indicated, are taken from THE HOLY BIBLE, NEW INTERNATIONAL VERSION®, NIV® Copyright © 1973, 1978, 1984, 2011 by Biblica, Inc. Copyright © 1982 by Thomas Nelson, Inc. Used by permission. All rights reserved.

Some scripture quotations are taken from New King James Version®. Copyright © 1982 by Thomas Nelson, Inc. Used by permission. All rights reserved worldwide.

If you wish to contact me about anything in the book please contact:

theadventureoffaith@hotmail.com

CONTENTS

Introduction and Acknowledgements   7

1. Faith - A Real Thing   9
2. The Wilderness of Faith   20
3. Faith and Logic   38
4. Faith and Living from the Tree of Life   49
5. When God Says No   64
6. Revelation & Condemnation   73
7. Faith & Finance   90
8. Knowing the Goodness of God   115

Final Thoughts   131

INTRODUCTION AND ACKNOWLEDGEMENTS

I have been thinking about writing a book for a couple of years now. I had ideas but every time I tried to write, it felt like I was trying to make something happen that just wasn't quite there. Then, just after Christmas last year, I felt God tell me to write a book on faith. Could that really be you, God? As I started to write on the subject, I found the words flowed from my heart. It was actually something that was quite easy for me to write. But, the stories and understanding have come from years of learning to hear God's voice and walk in faith, sometimes through great trials and difficulties.

Often people will ask someone how long it takes to prepare for a message or to write a piece of work. The reality is that sometimes things can take only a short time to write out, but the real question is, "How long have you carried this in your heart?" This is how this book has felt for me. It was actually something that was quite easy for me to write, but the stories and understanding come from years of learning to keep in step with God in the area of faith. I don't pretend to have all authority on the subject of faith and have simply written within the areas that God has given me revelation. I hope that our family's faith would inspire others to have faith and watch God do incredible things, through the unseen and unknown and into the blessing and promises of God.

As I reflect I realise just how much of my Christian life has been a walk in faith. I am very grateful to my wife, Carolyn, who has been a trusting companion in the journey of faith. Many times it has been her faith that has pulled me along or caused me to look up and see God again. My children have also played a part in this journey of faith. At times they may have wished that Mum and Dad had been rich, but instead, hopefully they have experienced the richness of God in their lives. They have come to understand that when you are in need, you go to the Father of Heavenly lights who never changes. He is our provider and our everlasting light. I want to thank my family for going on this walk of faith with me. I also want to thank all the incredible Christian friends and family that have encouraged me to take the next step. There are days when faith seems a distant friend, but the help and support of the body of Christ has given me the strength to go again. An encouraging word, a laugh, or simple prayer has lifted my eyes to the hills again to see my help coming from the Lord.

My hope is that you may get some encouragement, inspiration and hope as you read the words in these pages. My desire is that this book would be a book of life. That it would touch your heart and cause you to become free in some area of your life and, most of all, cause you to draw close to your Heavenly Father, knowing that he WILL COME THROUGH FOR YOU. Always and forever.

I hope you enjoy this book and experience the love of the Father through its pages.

Godspeed… James.

CHAPTER 1:
FAITH - A REAL THING

Many people see faith a bit like wishful thinking. If they can believe for something enough, then it will happen. Let me tell you that faith is much more than wishful or positive thinking. In **Hebrews 11:7** it says that "***faith is the substance** of things hoped for*" and I believe that is a pretty good description of what faith is. It is a substance, a real thing, a transaction between you and the Father. Something that was initiated in the heart of the Father before time began and that is now in your heart. When I first became a Christian, I was confused because faith almost sounded like positive thinking to me. If I believed in something enough then it would happen. I remember attending a new believer's course at my first church and a man in the audience asked why he hadn't yet received the red car that he had been believing for. Now I don't know that young man's heart and his request was not wrong. However, this example is how I believe we see faith sometimes; a list of requests that we initiate with God and according to our timing. But faith is not initiated in us but in Him. In **Romans 10:17** it says that "***faith comes from hearing, and hearing by the word of God***". When our faith comes from hearing God, we can be certain that he will bring it to pass.

Faith is initiated in the heart of the Father and when we get a hold of it we can not simply move it to one side. It will remain in us until he brings it to pass in this life or after you have gone. Faith is a real transaction between God and us. Abraham did not wake up one day and decide that he would be the Father of our Faith. He did not decide that he would have descendants as numerous as the sand on the seashore or that his wife would have a miracle child in her old age. God decided this long before Abraham was around. It was Abraham's job to discover what God had planned for him and continue to believe that He would see it through.

Think of God's first interaction with Jeremiah. After God affirms Jeremiah as a prophet and that he has set him apart from birth for God's purposes, he then shows him what it is to walk in faith. **In Jeremiah 1:11,** we see an initial interaction between God and Jeremiah that in some ways appears to serve no purpose.

> *The word of the Lord came to me: "What do you see, Jeremiah?"*
> *"I see the branch of an almond tree," I replied.*
> *The LORD said to me, **"You have seen correctly, for I am watching to see that my word is fulfilled".***

Now what was the purpose of God showing Jeremiah the branch of an almond tree? Only to show Jeremiah that he could see as God sees and when he later showed him something of significance, he would know he was seeing what God was showing him and could move in accordance with this. God goes on to speak to Jeremiah a second time. This time it is a word of faith that will indeed be fulfilled. He has seen correctly with the almond tree so he can now in faith see what God is wanting to do in the future.

> **Jeremiah 1:13-15:**
> *The word of the Lord came to me again: **"What do you see?"***

> *"I see a pot that is boiling,"* I answered. *"It is tilting toward us from the north.*
> *The Lord said to me, "From the north disaster will be poured out on all who live in the land. I am about to summon all the peoples of the northern kingdoms,"* declares the Lord.

God was watching to see if Jeremiah would see as He sees and whether the word he initiated was going to be fulfilled. This is how faith works – God initiates a word in our hearts through faith, just like he did with Jeremiah, and then He waits to see what we will do with it. Do we dismiss it, or like Jeremiah do we say, "I see what you are seeing, Lord. I believe that you will fulfil this word"? We can have faith in many things - ourselves, other people, luck, fate, the universe etc, but the faith that God recognises is that which has come from Him. He will back up His words and make sure they come to pass. In faith we see what God wants to do long before we see it happen. Faith is a real interaction between us and the Father, just as it was with Jeremiah.

When we lived in Tauranga NZ, just after my wife and I got married, I used to drive around in a Toyota Corona station wagon. I loved that car and it was the last manual car I ever owned. It was diesel and it would go for miles and miles before it needed fuel again. Because of finances, and the fact my wife didn't drive a manual car, we decided to downsize to one car and get rid of my Corona, upgrading to a much newer car that was automatic. The only problem was that when we started thinking about doing this we had no money for it as we were living off one income. During this time we had a very small car dealer at the end of our street and when I would leave for work in the morning I would pass a silver

Subaru station wagon sitting for sale outside the car yard. I can still remember the day when I drove past that car and I felt the small voice of God say to my heart, "You are going to have that car". Everyday from then on I would drive past that car and thank God for it, even though we did not have the money to buy it. One day, I came home and turned the corner and was astonished to see that the car yard was completely empty. In the time that I had been at work that day, every car had been relocated somewhere and the business had closed down. My silver Subaru was gone. However, when God reveals that he is going to give us something he delivers on his promise but not always in the way we expect. This is not wishful thinking but getting in line with the good, pleasing and perfect will of God for us. Not too long after that car yard closed down we finally got the money to buy a vehicle. I went down to a local auction place and when I arrived my eyes were drawn instantly to a silver automatic Hyundai station wagon, just like the one I had driven past all those times. I knew immediately that this was the car he had chosen for us. I struck a deal with the owner and drove off with a big smile on my face knowing that I had seen what the Father had seen all those months ago and his promise was now fulfilled. Faith is not some mumbo jumbo thing and it's not just given to positive people. It's a transaction that is available to all of us. It is a reflection of God's heart towards us and our reward for seeking him.

In **Hebrews 11:6** it says that, "*without faith it is impossible to please God*, because anyone who comes to him must believe that he exists and that he **rewards those who earnestly seek him**." Part of faith is earnestly seeking God and knowing that what he has for us is good. Seeking God is the first step in faith. When we lack a vision or any kind of hope we need to seek him with all our heart, knowing that vision and hope will soon flow.

A couple of years after becoming a Christian, I felt called to go to Faith Bible College in NZ. At the time I was living in Sydney and knew little about NZ except that it was where God was calling me. What really appealed to me about the bible college diploma was being able to complete a ten week mission in any field of ministry service that we wished and in any location. I had dreams of going somewhere with my surfboard under my arm and grabbing a quick surf in between ministry, but God had other ideas. I began to earnestly seek God, asking him where I should go. I was a young man who loved travelling to overseas countries and I dreamed of some exotic location. Many options were thrown up over the next weeks including the opportunity to go to Indonesia with one of the bible college lecturers. Again I could picture myself racing down to the surf in my spare time. But I had no peace in my heart to go to Indonesia or several other places where opportunities existed. As time drew closer to the beginning of our mission, a man came from India to our bible college and told us about his ministry and orphanage in India. I loved the idea of going to India and working with the children but after discussing it with the Pastor and praying about it, it just did not seem right to me. Something was uneasy in my Spirit, despite it ticking all the boxes. I was tempted to just go with it since it wasn't long until our plans needed to be finalised. However, I decided to step out in faith and say no and continue to seek God. Faith always comes with a sense of peace in our hearts. It may not always seem logical and we may have many questions about it, but faith always comes with peace. When we settle with a decision solely based on it being the right logical fit for us, we can often miss out on the faith journey that God desires.

CHAPTER 1

Just a few weeks after the visit from the Indian pastor, we went out on what was called Church Serve. This was where we went out on a Sunday and served at various churches in teams of bible college students. Often we would be asked to run the service, as we were on this occasion. This church was quite a traditional church with most of the congregation over retirement age. The service seemed to go ok, but little did I know that God was setting me up this day. After the service I was approached by a lady who must have been the youngest person in the church. She began to talk to me and quickly turned the conversation to an Indian orphanage and mission that she had started, asking whether I would like to visit one day. My spiritual antenna rose up and I knew God had spoken. I did not have to think too hard about this as I had an instant peace and felt a 'yes' in my heart to go as part of our mission service. At this time there were only a few weeks until our mission was going to commence and, as usual, God turned up right on time. That mission trip ended up being a foundational trip for me. Not only did I have a fantastic time with the children at the orphanage telling them bible stories, singing and playing cricket and all manner of games, but I also realised God had a call on my life. I knew that I would be asked to preach at churches and on the plane over I had written a couple of simple messages. Little did I know that I would clock up nearly 30 messages in the next month. On one Sunday I preached four messages at four different churches. The pastor would double me on his motorbike from one church to another. I had no idea how long I would need to preach or the size of the group where we were going. I would often turn up mid-service and they would stop whatever was going on to let the bible college student preach. I would then ask who wanted prayer, to which most of the church would come forward. I would literally pray for hundreds of people, laying my hands on each person for just a few seconds before moving to the next. It was then back on the motorbike and off to the next church. We preached in tiny community churches in small grass huts and bigger churches in large concrete buildings, containing several hundred people. It was a complete journey in faith and no amount of preparation could prepare me for it. On one occasion I preached in a village to a group who could neither read nor write and lived in simple shacks. I was later told that they were Hindus with hundreds of gods and one of these 'gods' was the tree I was leaning on. I had used it as a prop for describing the tree of the knowledge of good and evil from which Adam and Eve ate. There was no light so my notes were useless. I would think about what I might say during the time the pastor was translating it. On that occasion the small family group all stood up and said they wanted to follow Christ.

Faith is a real thing, a real transaction between you and the Father, one that has a real outcome. But God will allow us to follow our own desires and direction if we insist. The cry of Jesus' heart is expressed so well in **Luke 18:8** when Jesus asks, *"When the Son of Man comes, will he find faith on the earth?"* When Jesus finds people listening to him, believing in his word and continuing to believe his word despite the weight of evidence against something happening, I believe he is amazed. The story of the centurion highlights this so well. The centurion came to Jesus believing that he could heal his servant. When Jesus asked him if he should come to his home he said that he did not deserve this, but Jesus' word alone would be enough to bring healing to his servant. *"When Jesus heard this, he was amazed and said to those following him, '**Truly I tell you, I have not found anyone in Israel with such great faith**'"* (**Luke 7:9**).

Jesus was amazed and said that he had not seen such great faith amongst the Jews in Israel. To believe in the power and the character of Jesus when the odds are stacked against an event is rare and amazes even God. When was the last time Jesus was amazed by your faith? When he returns he will ask us – did you believe me? Did you act like you believed me? Did you live like I really existed?

When we were team leaders at a Youth With A Mission (YWAM) base in the South Island of NZ, we would run six month Discipleship Ministry Schools. These were essentially short term mission schools split up into two phases - the lecture phase, where students would come to know God more, and the outreach phase where they would make him known to others. Most of the students were between the ages of 18 and 30, but we had students of all ages. The outreach phase consisted of students going to multiple countries, serving and ministering in schools, orphanages, churches, and in the community. Many people who came to YWAM were able to pay for the lecture phase but needed some funds for the outreach component. This was not discouraged because part of people's growth in coming to YWAM was in believing God for funds and watching him provide, often in miraculous ways. In one school I was involved in we saw $65 000 provided in just a few days. Most students, however, did come with some sort of plan on how they might fundraise for outreach. Often students would have supportive family members and churches back home who were happy to give to them so they could go on their outreach. This wasn't always the case and God would provide in all manner of ways, but often through other students and staff. As the outreach component got closer our treasurer would summon students to his office to ask them about their funds for outreach and how they were intending to get them. His role as the accountant meant he needed to be far more pragmatic than the leaders of the base and schools. He was dealing with the facts and figures of what we actually had, while we often spent our time believing that God would provide even if it was at the 11th hour. In all my time as leader we never had to stop anyone going on outreach due to lack of funds, but we came close on several occasions.

One incident that taught me a lot about faith and how it might amaze God involved one young man from America who completed one of the schools. When he met with the treasurer he had not one dime for his outreach fees. The treasurer asked him how he intended to get these and he replied, "I don't know." The treasurer turned back to the young man and said in a matter of fact way, "Then how do you intend to go on outreach?"

"I don't know," said the young man, "All I know is that my sister had a dream that all of my outreach funds were provided and I could go to outreach."

This young man had come to YWAM believing that God would provide his outreach fees based on the fact that his sister had a dream in which all his finances were provided. The logical person in me thought it was almost unfair that this young man should come to YWAM and not pay a cent towards his outreach fees whilst many others had worked several jobs before coming to get the money together. It almost seemed lacking in wisdom and good sense. But as I prayed about it I was reminded of Jesus' amazement when the centurion had actually believed in what he could do for him. I began to see this young man through different eyes and that he was actually exercising great faith. He was not expecting others to provide for him and I'm sure he would have accepted the decision for him not to come on outreach if that was decided, but he was believing that God would fulfil his sister's dream. The next time I saw him I asked if he would be prepared to share the dream with all our base staff and students. He agreed and at our prayer time for finances he shared the dream with the whole group, including staff. That morning people responded to his faith with great generosity, pledging funds to help him go on outreach. All of this young man's fees were provided in one morning and it brought great joy to me to see his faith rewarded by God. God had decided long before that day that he was going to provide all his outreach fees. God's promise was passed to this young man's heart through his sister's dream and it then went through all the staff and students on base as they caught his faith. Faith is contagious and is often caught more than taught. At times it is amazing even for God that someone might believe that he will do what he says he will do.

Faith is a real thing that is passed from God's heart to ours. Its source does not come from us and is not about believing in ourselves or positive thinking. It is about hearing God's voice and believing what he has told us and moving in that direction. Expecting that if we position ourselves for what he has said, it will happen. With God I use the saying that we need to be, 'in the right place at the right time'. Have you ever tried to make something happen but it just didn't seem to be the right time? Maybe it's not the right time. That is how faith operates. God has a specific timing when he will fulfil his promise and we need to be in the right place at the right time to receive it.

Sometimes faith means we need to be acting like something is going to happen long before it actually happens. In other words, prepare for rain long before it rains. I love the story of Angus Buchan, the South African farmer who planted potatoes in a time of great drought in South Africa. He did this because he believed

God told him to do it despite there being no logic behind his decision. All the other farmers had chosen not to plant potatoes, an act of wisdom indeed. But sometimes faith will trump wisdom. The wise thing was not to plant potatoes, but God said do it anyway. I'm not talking about rash and silly decisions that we make on our own that supersede wisdom. These will lead to no good thing. I'm talking about our ability to choose what God has said over what the weight of evidence might suggest will happen. This is faith. Angus Buchan's decision to listen to God's voice over all the other voices of wisdom came with great risk. What would happen if there were no potatoes at the end of the harvest? Would this decision send him broke? If God did not come through this time, could he trust God the next time he heard his voice? For those that have seen the movie of this man's life, called 'Faith like Potatoes', you will know that Angus does end up with an amazing harvest of beautiful big potatoes. This is after a time of extreme drought in the land. Only God could do that. That is the power of faith.

Faith is real. Faith is us discovering the plans that God has for us and then believing them long enough to see God fulfil them. We don't make up faith or speak it into existence. God has already spoken it into existence and our job is to continue to believe him despite the circumstances. **Hebrews 11:6** reminds us that "*faith is the evidence of things not seen*". In other words, when faith comes it is the evidence that God is going to do what he says. This thing in our heart is a real thing and not a false hope or simply wishful thinking but the dreams of God coming alive and being worked out in our own hearts.

CHAPTER 2:
THE WILDERNESS OF FAITH

The book of Hebrews has a chapter that speaks about the heroes of faith. Many of us would like to be heroes of the faith, but faith has a cost. For some it was persecution, but for others it was simply waiting in a wilderness for the promise to come. Loren Cunningham the founder of Youth with a Mission (YWAM) wrote a book titled, 'Is that really you God?' When we choose to walk in faith we might often ask the question, "is that really you God?"

Often when God makes a promise to us it seems like a *fait accompli* that it will be done. But when we are left waiting for longer than we expect or things take a detour, we are tempted to lose heart or take matters into our own hands. We often use Abraham as an example of someone who took matters into his own hands and tried to speed up the wilderness of faith. But the truth is most of us would have been tempted to do the same thing. After all, Abraham and Sarah waited 25 years for God to give them a son and you could forgive Abraham for asking, "Is that really you God?"

When we stand in the gap between God's promise and reality, it often feels like a wilderness. Like a ship at sea, often we are close to land but it feels like we are in the middle of nowhere. The wilderness of faith, between the promise and the blessing, can be a tough place. You will be tempted to think that maybe you didn't hear God after all, maybe you will want to quit or try and speed up the process. Waiting with complete confidence is not easy and most of us will want to go back to God like a child would go back to their parents, wanting constant reassurance.

Carolyn and I got to witness a miracle when we lived in NZ with the purchase of our first home. Yet through this we also witnessed in some small way what Abraham might have experienced when he tried to make the miracle happen himself. It gave me a fresh understanding of the temptation he faced when he stood in the gap between faith and the blessing. Over the years we had tried several times to save up for a deposit for a home. On each occasion God would lead us into a new venture that would require us to use the funds we had accumulated. When God called us to Youth with a Mission in 2011, we had begun saving towards a home but to turn our back on what we felt God was calling us to was never an option. So the money we had saved went towards getting us to YWAM and paying our fees. In a way, we then resigned ourselves that, barring a miracle, we may never own our own home. I had never really had a strong desire to own my own home but as God blessed our family with children, this desire became very strong. Still, we had been called into mission work; paying the bills and enjoying anything extra God gave us seemed like all we could really ask for. But not long after we started working for YWAM as full time volunteers in 2011 Carolyn made the statement, "God is going to get us a house."

"Yes dear," was my response, wondering how that could ever happen. Then she came home early one day in 2015 declaring that she had found the house for us and that God was going to provide it for us. This sounded like a dangerous declaration of faith and one that I was going to get towed along with, as I had little faith of my own for this at the time. So at my wife's request, I went off to the bank with exactly zero dollars in savings and some bank records that showed that people had been giving us enough money to pay for rent, groceries, petrol etc., and that I had a very small income at the local school where I was doing youth work. As expected, I came back with my tail between my legs after the bank had offered us a loan of about $70 000, enough to buy a really fancy garden shed for our growing family of small kids. Now that I had proven to my wife that we were not going to be buying a home, I could go back to paying rent and not have to hope for something that was out of our reach. Yet Carolyn would not give up – "God's going to get us a house." It seems I couldn't get her off my back, just yet.

Over the next several months I tried lots of different things – other banks, building societies and high interest rate loan companies. We even asked some friends for interest free loans. Eventually a couple of our very good friends agreed to loan us the money, but as we began to get into the ins and outs of it, we realised that this was not going to be the right thing either. It's worth noting that whilst all this was going on, the house that Carolyn had said God was going to give to us had since had three offers made and all three had fallen through. We decided to make the fourth offer as this must be God. So we prayed, asked friends, sought counsel, and believed God that he would do an 11th hour miracle, but he didn't and our offer fell through too. Did God really say that he was going to get us a house? This question went through my mind and I was tired and frustrated. I felt completely powerless in the situation.

The only good thing that came out of this period of time is that friends caught Carolyn's faith and said they wanted to help us raise a deposit. Through the generous gifts of family and friends, we raised about $85 000 for a deposit. There were over 40 people who gave to us and the gifts ranged from $20 to $20 000. When people catch wind of faith they will naturally want to be part of it too. Maybe, to begin with, you will be walking alone, perhaps even walking through the wilderness like Abraham, but eventually you'll be surrounded by others who catch the faith that you are carrying.

After about six months we had a deposit but absolutely no hope of getting a loan and I felt like I had explored every avenue. It was nearly time to give up. I began to understand a little of what Abraham must have felt when year after year Sarah did not get pregnant. Maybe God needs a little help in the process? After all, one of our favourite sayings is that 'God loves those who help themselves'. Perhaps it's time to give him some help. About this time I felt sure that God was somewhere in this process, but even if we were just a few kilometres from shore, I could have been in the middle of the ocean. It felt like this was never going to come to pass. So I was getting desperate and one day I saw a thing come up on my screen that said I could earn $150 000 in a short amount of time. Maybe this was the thing that could get us out of trouble but it sounded too good to be true and was surely a scam, right? In my desperation, I emailed the link but didn't think much of it. By the way, I never do things like this. I'm the guy that hangs up on salesmen. So within one minute my phone rings from Britain. I knew the country code because I lived there for two years. It was an Israeli guy and it sounded like he was in a very noisy place which he described to be the London stock exchange and I actually believe it was. He began to talk to me about this scheme and told me to just put in $250 to begin, which was all we had in our account anyway.

"You've got nothing to lose, you will gain money almost certainly, and by the way how's your family, who is your favourite football team? Take your time to think about this, but if you put the money in right now I'll put a matching bonus amount in for you."

Now this guy is just about the best and nicest salesman that I have ever met and you couldn't help but warm to him. He makes me want to instantly buy in but I manage to hold him off for a short time so I can talk to my wife.

"What, your wife? Let me talk to her," the salesman exclaims and he sweetly talks to her as well.

"I'll call you back," I say.

"Ok but my bonus offer will only last an hour," he finishes, clearly trying to get me to buy in instantly. In the midst of all that was going on and in my desperation, I hit the pay credit card to put my first $250 into the account. That would pretty soon transform into $150 000 once this stockbroker had finished with my money. Annoyingly it's $250 US and not $250 NZD, as I had assumed, and there is not enough money in my account. So I can't pay but I now have time to research the company a bit. It turns out they are not a fully fledged scam, just a very unscrupulous company with hundreds of stories of people struggling to reclaim their money and losing it . Afterwards, I realised that I had dodged a bullet when the money did not go through. The salesman continued to ring me for the next week and after I ignored about ten phone calls he finally got the message and left me alone.

What was the moral of that story? Just that I could understand how Abraham might have been so desperate to see God's word fulfilled that he thought he and Sarah could help him a bit. And it would still be faith and it would still be God, just with a bit of help. So they decided to arrange for Hagar, Sarah's maid servant, to sleep with Abraham. Sure enough it works and they have a child and they name him Ishmael. But there is only one problem, this child was made from their own schemes and ideas and is not the child of God's promise. Ishmael is not the child of faith that Abraham and Sarah were waiting for. But God is still faithful despite their unfaithfulness and impatience. Finally, after 25 years God's word is fulfilled with the birth of Israel to Sarah at a very old age. And just like Abraham, my dealings with the Israeli salesman hadn't come from faith but through impatience to see God's word fulfilled. Waiting in the wilderness of faith, the gap between promise and receiving is a place that we don't like to live in for too long and at times we would all like to give God a little hurry on. Yet when God does act it will happen quickly, but in his time. In **Isaiah 60:21-22** it speaks of a prophecy about Israel being restored and it finishes with this statement: *"I am the Lord, **in its time I will do this swiftly**"*. When God moves he will move quickly, but his timing in faith is everything and we need to move in his time, Godspeed.

Finally, we did get a house. Not the same one that Carolyn had wanted at first but something way more practical and enjoyable for our needs. How did we get the money? Well I had already mentioned about the deposit coming from friends, but after much exploring and just waiting on God to show us how, a friend suggested we contact the bank manager who had managed our YWAM base accounts for the last few years, as he would know a bit more about who YWAM was. Hopefully he might even count our gift payments from others as income. We had already been rejected by his bank but I hadn't thought to go directly to him. So, after meeting with him, he agreed to loan us more than enough to purchase our first home and what a miracle home it was. We could have spoken to him as our first person but here we were, almost a year later, when we got a simple idea from a friend and God turned up for us. Looking back, you can't help but smile at the faithfulness and generosity of God, but honestly the process I have just described took about 18 months to see the promise fulfilled. It pales in comparison to Abraham and Sarah's 25 years, but for us it felt like a long time in a wilderness of waiting. The time was long enough for us to ask the question, "Is this really you God?", to want to give up on the process and to definitely hit walls that to us looked like permanent endings. But faith is God's battle that we get to fight with him. This was his way of winning the battle and there was no way we could take any credit for it. The only thing we can ever claim when we walk in faith is that we endured and did not give up – isn't that the one thing that God commends his people on in the bible? In **Revelation 3:8**, God says through the prophet John, *"I know you have little strength, yet you have kept my word and have not denied my name."* God plays the major part in faith and he knows that we have little strength, but he commends us for not giving up. Don't give up if you are in the wilderness of waiting and don't try to speed up the process, although it probably doesn't hurt to ask God if he could speed it up :-)

It's also worth noting here that to live in faith does not necessarily have to mean living in lack. For us, many of our encounters with the miraculous and faith have come because of our lack of resources. We have six children and worked in a mission organisation and in Youth Work for about seven years. During that time we needed to trust God for finance and that created an open door for faith adventures. Faith is seeking God, hearing God and acting or moving according to his word. Acts of faith also involve us giving according to God's leading and we have been part of these times too. Joseph was called by God to save Egypt's resources (grain) for seven years (**Genesis 41**). He did this because he heard God and interpreted a dream for Pharaoh. This was indeed an act of faith. Firstly, if things didn't go as planned, according to his interpretation of Pharaoh's dream, he may have lost his head. Secondly, his interpretation was not directly in favour of God's people but it was in the favour of a pagan nation. This act would potentially give Egypt the power to dominate the then known world and enslave the Israelites, which of course they later did under the Pharaoh's son's rule. Joseph would not have known at the time how this act of faith might benefit his family and the nation of Israel. He would not have been able to see that by listening to God he would save his family's life and would allow a season in history where Israel was able to flourish side by side with a Pagan nation.

However, sometimes our lack or need does provide the perfect conditions for faith. After all, when we are lacking in an area of our life we earnestly seek God, which **Hebrews 11** describes as being part of the process of faith. This lack could be in any area of our life where we need God's intervention or provision. It may be in our relationships, our emotional state or simply to see a dream of God that has been birthed in us come true. In **Hebrews 3:11, Romans 1:17** and **Galatians 3:11** it says that *"the righteous' shall live by faith"*. Faith is the economy of God and it is the connection of our heart to him. No matter what level of resources or need we are in, we are called to live by faith. We are called to live by the unseen and not the seen, to live by the word of God. We are told in **Matthew 4:4** that *"we do not live on bread alone but on every word that comes from the word of God"*. In other words we are called to live by faith and not just by what we see in front of us right now. Faith is initiated by God, but we have a responsibility to stir that faith up, reminding our hearts of what God has said and creating an atmosphere for others to enter into this faith that we carry.

One other example in our lives where we saw the delay of God and wondered if indeed this was really him, involved the birth of our daughter Genesis. We have five incredible boys in our home and I love each of them with all my heart, but long before four of those boys were born we felt that God was going to give us a girl. My wife has always had a very prophetic gift in that she sees things in the Spirit that are coming and declares them before they arrive. Before each of our children were born she had a clear sense that she was to give them a very specific name. We never had any problem naming our kids because Carolyn had received their names in faith long before they were born and I simply agreed with her faith. When we received the name Genesis we expected that she would be next along. However, we were in for a surprise…

The backstory to that story was that when we first got married Carolyn spent two years at Faith Bible College. Due to a variety of reasons, Carolyn was reluctant to have children. So it came as a great surprise to me one day when she came home from a mission trip in Samoa, telling me that we were going to have a son called Titus. Whilst reading her bible one morning the name 'Titus' stood out to her as to what we should call our first child. This was a word of faith for her, as up until this point children were not on her agenda. Not long after she returned home she was praying with a beautiful Korean lady at College who became excited in the Spirit as she could see Carolyn with a little baby boy. She declared that Carolyn was going to have a child soon. Carolyn caught this faith immediately and this lady's faith now became Carolyn's and she came home to tell me, which in turn gave me the faith to believe that this was now the season for us to have our first child. When they were praying the lady said she also saw a girl but that she was off in the distance, a long way off. So when she got pregnant the second time, we both assumed that a baby girl was on the way. Then only about a month before the baby was born, Carolyn received the name 'Zephyr' and said she felt that this baby could actually be a boy. Indeed it was a beautiful boy, Zephyr. We then had another boy, Leeland. After this Carlolyn got the name Genesis and we were now confident that we would meet her next. But a wonderful surprise followed, two more boys, Samson and Moses. By this stage we had five children, two miscarried babies, and a whole range of emotional, financial and relationship challenges going on. I want to clarify now that we never kept having children because we wanted to have a girl, as many people assume. We kept having children because each time in faith Carolyn would get a name from God and we knew this was a little life that he wanted to birth through us. But after five kids and all the pressures that were on our lives it was pretty obvious that we could not bear much more. However, after stepping down as leaders of the YWAM base in NZ, we felt called to rest and refresh at a YWAM family ministry school in Norway. Whilst we were there we had time to reflect on the last few chaotic and difficult years. Five children in a short season and the pressures of leading a YWAM base in transition had come at a cost to us. We needed rest and healing and the thought of another child was not in our planning. However, when we thought about Genesis, we realised that she was not just a name but that she was a child who we believed was going to be entrusted to us. God had not forgotten Genesis or his promise to us. She had come from a download of faith to our hearts and could not just be pushed to the side. God would deliver what he had promised.

So despite the fact we were so overloaded by life when we arrived in Norway, we both agreed that another season of child birthing in three plus years was unbearable to think about. It was now or never for us. We knew that others, with good reason too, would not understand why we would want to have another child with all the pressures that we were currently facing. But we knew what God was saying. Eight years after Carolyn had first seen that little girl in the Spirit, God fulfilled his promise of a beautiful girl to us. Having six children so close together like we have had has brought immense pressure and challenges for us as a family. I wouldn't describe it as material to place in a family planning book to help new parents, but I would describe it as the journey that God chose for us and an amazing walk of faith with him.

Carolyn's Story of Faith

I never thought I would have children. It just never was something I thought about. Even the idea of getting married only changed when I felt a shift and all of a sudden it was like God showed me that I could get married and that the person was James. Even in our beach walk chats I still remember telling James I didn't think I'd have kids.

But that would all change...

After a very stressful year of being a full time teacher in my first year out of college, I met James and we were married during the last week of school. My job had been a one year relief position to replace the Head of Art, who was taking time out to study. I also gave my life back to God during this time, so that also came with a huge shift in areas that needed to be left behind. The following year I was excited to attend the Bible College which my now husband had gone to, prior to meeting me.

So I embarked on this new journey, learning to hear God's voice for myself and having this bold new relationship with him. Prior to this I had felt that God was faraway, sitting somewhere up in the sky only to come down occasionally.

In my second year of bible college we had the opportunity to go on an outreach of our own choosing and the timing was perfect for me to go to Samoa. This was with an organisation with whom my parents had been heavily involved in when I was a young girl. Word of Life was focused on equipping its students with understanding the word of God and it was through this ministry that our family came from Australia to New Zealand to start the ministry there.

My heart was so soft as a child and I had flourished being a part of a faith community. Going to the holiday camps held life-long memories. One of the founding staff members who also had been like an uncle to me and my sisters was leading the group, so it was super special.

It was during that trip while sitting on the beach having a quiet time and looking over the clear blue waters of Samoa that I heard the inner voice of God as clear as though someone

CHAPTER 2

spoke to me. All he said was, "Titus!" Instantly at that moment, I knew that I would have a child and he would be called Titus!!

I don't remember how James reacted when I told him back at home, but soon after during a prayer time in our chapel at bible college I shared this name with a trusted friend. She prayed with me about this idea of having a child. We both saw the same picture, a little boy with light coloured hair and a little girl in the background further off. This felt like another promise; not only that I would have a son but also a daughter.

Soon after we were expecting Titus, and I would spend many hours sitting and praying over our child growing strong inside. While holding him after giving birth, this soft squishy little babe, I couldn't help but keep repeating, "I can't believe it's Titus, I cant believe it's Titus!" I marvelled at this new creation before me.

Three months later we headed off to the South Island of NZ, packing up all we owned to attend a Youth With A Mission (YWAM) school. The school was put on hold for three months so we were able to spend this time with my parents in their cottage at Nelson. Becoming a new mum and then moving had its challenges and Titus wasn't a settled baby, so there were lots of firsts to work through. To say I often felt out of my depth was an understatement. Many moments were spent crying out to God to come into my feelings of *inadequacy as a mum.*

During the next season, as we were immersed in the YWAM school there was again a shift in my spirit. My eyes were opened to this new understanding and knowing that the God of the universe was not only the one who had created the world but he was also my Father with the heart of a mother. This was a new way of relating to God as a perfect parent. He knew all my failings, loved me despite them, and still said I was worthy to be a mother.

Two years after Titus we welcomed Zephyr, named after Zephaniah whom I had learned at Bible College meant 'hidden treasure'. I had felt this name come two weeks before he was born, prior to that I thought we were going to be having our 'girl'. After all, I'd just seen two kids, so that seemed manageable right?! It seemed God had far greater plans than I could imagine.

Next came Leeland which meant 'green pastures', full of potential as in Psalm 23.

After Leeland I felt God gave me the name Genesis, a girl's name!! So when I fell pregnant next I thought this must be our last, a girl. But at my 13 week scan with my sister by my side the sonographer said, "I would expect to see the heartbeat after this many weeks but I'm not seeing it, I'm sorry." In my naivety I said, "Oh!? Will I need to come back?" When she didn't reply right away it felt like a part of my spirit was

CHAPTER 2

crushed and fell away as reality rushed up to meet me. My sister and I sat in disbelief in the car park as to what had just happened; neither of us had any experience with miscarriage. We just sat and cried, not really knowing what to do next. What followed was a mixture of experiencing both the confusion of loss and the wonder of God's creation.

My little babe didn't seem in a hurry to come out, so after spending a day waiting in gynaecology I was told they were overbooked and was sent home medicated to allow the process to happen naturally. I was terrified and many concerns were going through my mind, but a small mercy was given to me on both the way to and from the hospital. The song 'Noel' by Lauren Diagle was playing on the radio. This babe was not my Genesis, it was Noel, 'the first Christmas', the most treasured moment in time when our saviour God came down to earth, as a vulnerable babe. This was our Noel, our moment in time where God would make himself known intimately to me.

In the early moments of that morning, amongst the blood, came this perfect Thumbelina child, with ten fingers and toes and perfectly formed ears. I held her out to show James and I think there were murmurs of "oh, that's good dear," as he rolled back over to sleep. I felt like I was looking into a moment of time in creation, this moment that only a few see, where our Heavenly Father with the heart of a mother whispers to our open wounds and declares, "You needed to see this beauty in the brokenness." I gave this little forever Thumbelina a kiss and amid the tears declared "You are so, so beautiful! So so beautiful!" This understanding of the heart of God for us was made real, that there is nothing we could do more, or differently that would change this bond of LOVE that our Heavenly Father has always had for us. For before we were even formed in the womb he knew us, and chose us to be his kids.

My wounds didn't heal instantly. Not only did this make way for confusion and pain but so many questions flung within the tears at God. My physical body didn't mend well, and six weeks later I was again booked in to see the gynaecologist as there was retained placenta. Some weeks later I was still bleeding and I thought I was again miscarrying, but it was just more retained placenta. I felt like that woman who had touched the hem of Jesus' garment wanting to be healed. Again this reality of the hand of God was made evident as my body healed and my heart began to follow.

During the following days after the initial miscarriage I was in bed and too exhausted and fragile to go out. It was during this time that I felt God gave me the name 'Samson', which means 'sunshine'. I felt like this was God's promise of sunshine after the rain. I also had the name 'Moses' on my heart after watching *The Prince of Egypt* during those recovery days in bed. The name Moses means 'the one to lead the people'.

Samson was born and I was a mum now to four boys. I can't say this had ever been in my plans, but this one step at

CHAPTER 2

a time journey of faith with all its ups and downs was now my story.

During those years of 'littles', I struggled with deep depression, anxiety and this constant feeling of confusion looming over me. We weren't this cookie cutter clan but a tribe of misfits trying to keep instep with God's plans for our lives. Even if on the outside it seemed a bit out of the box, I think that's where God wants us to live, relying on his strength, direction and grace.

Pregnant with our fifth, I said I'm done, but deep down I knew God had not finished our journey of family. James had a dream one night and as I remember it was a picture of a young goat waiting on the other side of a gate to be let in. He felt like this was a picture of another child still waiting to come to us and I remember bursting into tears knowing this to be true.

We lost our next baby at 8 weeks. It was not the same shock I had experienced with our first loss, but was still an emotional time mixed with fear and remnants of my past experience. I got terrible morning sickness with each pregnancy, although I don't know why they call it 'morning sickness' when it lasts all day.

When we fell pregnant again, we both knew it was our last. Not only was I done physically but mentally and emotionally it felt like this journey had been a long one. Trusting in God's plans, even while struggling, can feel like you're going through a fog that you hope soon lifts.

Hearing "it's going to be a girl", at our scan felt surreal, as our promise of a girl was really here, though in many ways I couldn't quite believe it until she was in our arms. Genesis Beverly Joy was born nearly ten years after God first showed me that picture of a boy with a girl in the distance. Somehow, I felt like if he had shown me a picture of eight children I wouldn't have quite believed it, so instead he showed me something I could hold onto. If we have faith that feels small and if we plant it, keep watering it, and are faithful in what we can control, God has the pleasure of turning our little morsels of faith into fields of rich potential. To accomplish what God has set out for us to do and be a part of – that is the journey of faith. To not know the end and yet know that he is leading us all the way.

CHAPTER 3
FAITH AND LOGIC

Faith is much more than our logical beliefs. You can believe that something could happen but only in a theoretical sense. Faith is a deposit of hope and certainty that God plants in our hearts, that we are called to nurture until it is time for it to come into life. Faith is something we carry and take life defining steps to align our lives with. Having a theoretical belief about something does not bring power and authority, but faith comes with both power and authority. Even when a person speaks in faith, rather than just with a theoretical belief, you can feel the confidence behind their words. **Matthew 17:20** says, *"For truly, I say to you, if you have faith like a grain of mustard seed,* **you will say to this mountain, 'Move from here to there,' and it will move,** *and* **nothing will be impossible for you.**"

Faith gives us authority and power to command mountains to move from one place to another. These may not be actual physical mountains but Jesus is speaking to all kinds of barriers and challenges that may seem like blockages to receiving his blessing. When faith comes so does the ability to take authority over a situation. Faith enables you to complete a task at just the right time. For example, you may have ideas about something, but my experience is that those ideas will often just lie dormant with no power behind them, until you hear from God and move in faith. You now have the power to speak these things into being. Believing in something is not the same as faith because faith has God's 'power' and authority behind it.

> **Joshua 6:2-5**
>
> *And the Lord said to Joshua, "See! I have given Jericho into your hand, its king, and the mighty men of valour.* ***You shall march around the city, all you men of war; you shall go all around the city once. This you shall do for six days.*** *And seven priests shall bear seven trumpets of rams' horns before the ark.* ***But the seventh day you shall march around the city seven times, and the priests shall blow the trumpets.*** *It shall come to pass, when they make a long blast with the ram's horn, and when you hear the sound of the trumpet, that all the people shall shout with a great shout;* ***then the wall of the city will fall down flat.*** *And the people shall go up every man straight before him."*

Joshua and the Israeelites operated in much more than logical belief when the walls of Jericho fell down (**Joshua 6:1-21**). Joshua could have had a theory that the walls of Jericho could fall down if they walked enough steps and yelled loud enough, but he would have been a fool to attempt that simply because he believed that it could happen. However, his actions were not inspired by his theoretical belief about something but by the fact that he had heard God and he now had faith that God would do exactly what he had said he would. He now had confidence and certainty that God would come through. Faith comes with risk because, as the book of James says, it always comes with actions. Our logical beliefs can be very theoretical and people may be very outspoken in their beliefs – I know I can be. But just believing in something has no real power until it is accompanied by faith and then accompanied by the willingness to act. What God asked Joshua and the Israelite army to do is actually quite ridiculous as far as army tactics go. This was not about wisdom or belief but about doing what God was asking them to do in faith. The bible is full of the Father asking Jesus and other godly men and women to do things that may have seemed a little odd or foolish, even a little mad, but faith is about obedience and not about what we look like.

After we stood down as leaders of a YWAM base in NZ, we went and did a Family Ministry School in Norway (as I have previously mentioned). During this time we sought God as a couple and came back with the vision of becoming part of a Christian School in Australia, as a family. Before we could do this I had to get back into teaching in NZ. When we came home it was the middle of the school year and I was not in a good place to start full time teaching. So I did relief teaching for the remainder of the year, a process which comes with little stress but one that can feel meaningless. As the new year began to come into view and positions for the following year were to be advertised I had a sense from God that I was going to be working at my local school where my children went. Whenever I prayed about getting a job this was what came to mind. Then one day I was reading the story of the Israelites and Jericho from **Joshua 6** (see above) and I sensed this was quite a personal word for me in regard to the teaching position. The school where my kids were going had a very low turnover of staff in the grades I taught, as it was a country school and people moved to the school for the accompanying lifestyle. I felt like the Lord was encouraging me to pray that the walls of the school would come down, metaphorically, and there would be a flow of staff leaving and a group of new staff, including me, coming into the school. When I went to a men's group that I belonged to that same week I shared the scripture of the Israelites and Jericho and how I felt like it was a word for me. I said that I felt God was going to give me a job there, but that very few people in my year levels ever left. In a very quick summary, God asked Joshua and the Israelites to walk around Jericho every day for six days and on the seventh day they walked around Jericho seven times with great shouting and the blasting of trumpets. At this time the walls of Jericho would fall and they would be able to enter and defeat the enemy.

When I shared that I intended to walk around the school for seven days in the same manner that Joshua and the Israelites did, I was surprised that two of the men in my group said that they wanted to join me, essentially confirming that this felt like a word of faith to them. So each day that week I walked around the school praying and declaring that the walls would fall and positions would become vacant for myself and others who needed to be there. I was joined by men from the men's group on three of the days and walked a few days on my own, which was fine as I hadn't expected others to join me. On the seventh day my wife said that she and the whole family were planning to join me for the final seven laps. It was Sunday morning and I intended to go down after church that morning and complete the laps. When I awoke it was raining heavily, not a great day for a family walk. Yet we knew we had to finish what God had asked us to do, so in the pouring rain Carolyn and I walked with kids in strollers, on bikes and some walking. By halfway the novelty of riding in the cold and rain had worn off and the kids wanted to quit. I said that we had to finish what we started as this was what God wanted us to do. We managed to carry on and when we finished we let out a huge shout. No walls fell down that day but I believe something in the Spirit did. When we obey

God and do what he asks in faith, something happens in the Spirit realm. When God pruned Gideon's army back, from 22 000 to just 300 men, it wasn't a tactical move but a move to see if they would trust God (Judges 7). God's tactics are always victorious even if they involve a small boy with a slingshot and a few stones standing up against a giant in full armour. When we move with his Spirit, he takes care of the result.

After that day I felt confident that God was going to open up the job at my local school, but the job season passed and nothing became available. I ended up relief teaching for another term which is probably what I needed, as I still wasn't in a good place. I then found a contract for three terms to get me back into full time teaching, but I knew that God was going to open up that job for me at the local school. It took a year after we walked around the school for me to finally get that job. I can see why in many ways it didn't happen immediately, but I also believe that on the day we finished the seventh lap on the seventh day the deal was sealed and God would open up the door he had shown me. It took a year for this to happen but when it did there came a flow of people out of the school and a new flow of people in. What I had seen only in the Spirit a year before, now became a reality.

When it comes to acts of faith, sometimes people will question why you do not take the most logical and convenient path. Most of us will know the story of Gideon as a story of courage and trust but as a leader you would never teach anyone to cut their army from 32 000 to 300 soldiers. It defied all logic and good sense, but God wanted to show Gideon and the army that this was his battle. Faith is God's battle, it's not always logical or what we might think to be the best way, but it is God's way.

God showed me very early in my walk with him that the most convenient or logical way was not going to be the way he would lead me. He showed me this in his choice of bible college for me less than two years into my walk with him. At the time I was getting itchy feet in the job I was in. I was struggling being at a workplace where I felt like my gifts didn't really fit and it wasn't an encouraging environment to be in. I was working in a specialty school at the time for students who either weren't turning up to school or had been asked to leave one or more schools due to poor decisions. I look back now and can see it was a great time of learning and growth. I can see just how much God did while I was there, but it was an uncomfortable time in my life. After being in the job for just over twelve months I decided I was going to leave at the end of the year and go into Christian missions overseas. After all, I was single and without too many commitments. I can remember telling God that I was going to start to plan this and he would need to steer me on another course if he had other plans. I made plans to go on the weekend and start looking for airline flights. Just prior to the weekend I had a chiropractic appointment with a local man who I knew was a Christian. As he cracked and twisted my back that day for some reason he thought to tell me about a bible college he attended in the North Island of NZ, called Faith Bible College (FBC). I mentioned previously that what caught my ear about FBC was that they had a ten week mission component in the course where you could essentially choose where you wanted to go. Everything he told me that day about the college and even the town excited me and I walked out of that appointment knowing that I would be heading to Faith Bible College in NZ the following year. I never did get to the travel agents to seek flights, nor did I seek any other options. God had spoken and I was going. As the time got closer to leaving, many people asked me why I didn't go to the local bible college that was connected to the church I had found salvation in. Surely it was closer, cheaper and more convenient for me to go there. It's hard to explain faith to others and sometimes it's best not to. You may be misunderstood but you will have a massive amount of peace and excitement in your heart. Once you have heard God and faith has come into your heart it is impossible for someone to make you think differently about something. Faith is often not the most logical, the most practical or convenient way for you to do something. It is God's way and it's often totally outside of the box that you would have imagined it to be in. I have found just how amazing God is at taking us places that truly fulfil the desires of our heart. After all, this is the God who says that when we delight ourselves in him, he will give us the desires of our hearts **(Psalm 37:4)**. My experience at Faith Bible College changed my life and I would never be the same. It wrecked my ability to ever have a placid relationship with God ever again. I could not just sit still and go to church on a Sunday. I would go wherever he wanted me to go.

Faith and belief are different because belief can simply remain theoretical, which does not come from our heart. One of the most commonly used scriptures regarding salvation is from **Romans 10:9** where Paul says that when you *"confess with your mouth that Jesus is Lord and believe in your heart that God raised him from the dead, you will be saved."* I believe what Paul speaks of here is faith. When we believe something in our hearts, essentially it is faith. There are over 800 scriptures in the bible that speak about the heart. Not the beating, ticking thing that keeps us alive but the very centre of who we are. Many people see the heart as only the emotional centre of who we are. Yet the heart is much more than just emotion, it contains our spiritual life. The bible describes it as the "wellspring of life" **(Proverbs 4:23)**. It is our inner person, where our very spiritual life comes from. Our heart speaks of our truest desires and beliefs and we see that reflected in the scripture that says that when we *"delight ourselves in the Lord he will give us the desires of our heart"* **(Psalm 37:4)**. In other words our truest desires come from our heart, the very core of who we are. Many of our so-called desires come and go but the true desires of our heart remain until they are satisfied in faith. When we believe something in our hearts it is speaking of believing something with our truest self, not because we have to or because it is culturally acceptable or because it is logically right. We believe it because it resonates with our truest self, the deepest part of who we are. So when Paul speaks of believing something with our heart, I believe he is speaking about faith.

When I experienced salvation for myself I also got to experience the difference between just believing something in theory, compared to truly believing it in my heart. After I came back from travelling and living overseas for three years I reached a very lonely and unsatisfying time in my life. I started to seek God in some way but I couldn't give him my life or my heart because I didn't trust him to do something good with it. One Sunday night all my housemates had gone out for the night and I decided to visit the local church, which happened to be very large, one that some might describe as a mega church. I sat and listened that evening and was totally convicted by the Pastor's message and realised that I did indeed need God. When the time came for people to accept Christ as their saviour that night, a call was given to raise your hand if you wanted to do that. I raised my hand but very quickly and I made sure that it did not go above my head. When this time finished I realised that my half-a-hand up was sighted by one of the ushers and I was tapped on the shoulder to go down to the front and do business with God. I went down to the front of this huge church and I was surrounded by more than a hundred others, some helpers from the church, and some doing what I was doing. We were led in a prayer which I can only describe as something I said but did not mean in my heart. In other words it did not come from faith. After speaking to one of the church volunteers I went home, but I only felt a weight of depression and helplessness over me because I had not truly accepted Christ into my deepest person. I did not believe in Christ with all my heart, yet. Two weeks went past and I almost thought that maybe I could forget what I had done. Maybe it was a mistake that I had made and I could go on with my life, perhaps I could go travelling again, even though I had been homesick and desperate to come home to Sydney in my final months of living in the UK. At this time I was in a relationship with a person in the UK and I can honestly say that she was the biggest reason that I could not surrender my whole being to God. One night she rang me saying that she had great news, that she had accepted Christ as her saviour and felt like a new person, full of hope and joy. I had not discussed with her what had happened to me, so God was doing something totally separate here. Her story sounded much more like the 'good news' of salvation that is described in the bible and, without a doubt, it was also an act of faith for her in which she believed in Christ with her heart and could profess this with her mouth. This had not been my experience at all as I had not truly accepted Christ as my saviour. When I got off the phone to her that night I walked to my room and heard a word from God that helped me move from simply a theoretical belief to one of complete faith that Jesus was my Lord and Saviour. As I got to my room I heard an inner voice, which I later came to know as God's voice say, "I have taken out your last excuse, what are you going to do about it?" Those words brought down the last of my resistance and as I opened the door to my room I could hardly hold back the tears that were beginning to flow. I simply said, "I give up

Lord." The tears of resisting God for so long now poured down my face and his comfort began to flow into my heart. I now gave God my life to run as I wanted to give up being the leader of my life. Jesus Christ was now the leader and ruler of my heart. I had gone from a place of simply believing that God was real to a place of faith where I believed in him with my whole being and was ready to start trusting him with my life.

(I want to add that I later met Carolyn, my beautiful wife that I am married too today, but with her permission I shared this story to demonstrate how saving faith works.)

Faith always comes with an action and a response, sometimes even a change of course or direction. Faith is always more than a theoretical belief or having an opinion on something. In fact most of the time our opinion and walking in faith come from very different sources. Faith comes from hearing God but our opinion can often come from our own judgement on what we deem is 'right or 'wrong', (but more on that next chapter). The scripture in **James 2** that speaks about faith being accompanied by works is not just speaking about doing good things, as is often assumed. We can do many good things that are not inspired by a relationship with God and are not acts of faith. Good works of themselves are not necessarily what pleases God. **Hebrews 11:6** says that it is faith that pleases God. When we respond to what God is speaking in faith, this pleases him. When God shows you something you will want to respond from faith because a true heart surrendered wants to do what pleases their Father, as Jesus' did. The example given in **James 2** is actually about faith and how Abraham responds to this with action. Abraham decides to act upon his faith and take his very own son to the altar to offer him as a sacrifice. This seems very harsh but he later reveals that he is actually believing that God will provide another sacrifice in replacement of his son, to which of course he does. He only responds to God this way because he believes that this is what God is asking him to do in faith. It is not simply a 'good thing' to do, but a response to faith. It is not about him doing lots of things to please God, but pleasing God by responding to his faith with the appropriate action. Good works come from faith because faith always has an action. It is this faith that pleases God, but when we believe that God is only interested in our good works our hearts will never be at rest. We will run from one thing to the next in a vain attempt to please our Heavenly father.

CHAPTER 4
FAITH AND LIVING FROM THE TREE OF LIFE

In this chapter I want to speak about the two trees that were in the Garden of Eden and how much they have altered the way we live our lives. Most of us are aware of 'the fall' and how sin and death entered the world, but we are only just beginning to see how eating from the Tree of the Knowledge of Good and Evil caused mankind to live in an entirely different way and through an entirely different lens than was intended. I am indebted to James and Denise Jordan, founders of FatherHeart Ministries and other teachers in that ministry, for my ability to see faith and life in a new way. This understanding comes out of a teaching that is called 'The Two Trees' and it has been one of the most profound mysteries of God that I have ever come to discover in his word. To show how we can return to living through the lens of the tree of life and how this is connected to faith, I will need to explain this teaching further through **Genesis 2** and **3**.

As we all know there were many trees in the Garden of Eden but two trees are highlighted in God's word as being in the centre of the garden, presumably because they were significant and important for Adam and Eve. The first was the tree of life and the second was the tree of the knowledge of good and evil.

CHAPTER 4

Genesis 2:8-9
Now the Lord God had planted a garden in the east, in Eden; and there he put the man he had formed. The Lord God made all kinds of trees grow out of the ground—trees that were pleasing to the eye and good for food. **In the middle of the garden were the tree of life and the tree of the knowledge of good and evil.**

The tree of life was the tree that Adam and Eve ate from to remain in eternal life. This becomes clear after they sin, are driven from the garden, and a flaming sword and a cherubim are placed to guard the way to the tree of life. God says in **Genesis 3: 22** that man "*must not be allowed to reach out his hand and take also **from the tree of life and eat, and live forever.***" In other words, after the fall they could no longer eat from this tree and as promised in scripture they would now "*surely die*", instead of living forever. In light of this, God driving Adam and Eve from the Garden of Eden could be seen as an act of mercy because had they continued to eat from the tree of life they would have lived forever in their sinful state, as would we. Sin, sickness and death now became part of our reality and we commonly know this as 'the fall'. However, the tree of life is not inaccessible forever and it appears in **Revelation 22:2** when John is describing the New Jerusalem, our new heaven and earth. It is there on the sides of the river of the water of life for "*the healing of the nations*" and will allow us to live forever once again.

Genesis 3: 22-24
And the Lord God said, "The man has now become like one of us, knowing good and evil. **He must not be allowed to reach out his hand and take also from the tree of life and eat, and live forever."** *So the*

> *Lord God banished him from the Garden of Eden to work the ground from which he had been taken.* ***After he drove the man out, he placed on the east side of the Garden of Eden cherubim and a flaming sword flashing back and forth to guard the way to the tree of life.***

From now on when I speak of the tree of life it will be purely as a metaphor and in relation to the way Adam and Eve related to God prior to the fall. To live from the tree of life describes a way of relating to the Father and how we evaluate what is good and evil. In a way to live from the tree of life is to live from faith. It is going back to a way of living with God the Father before sin gripped humanity and we began predominantly living from the knowledge of 'good' and 'evil'. Living from the tree of life could be described as living from a place of meeting and hearing from God, as Adam and Eve did in the cool of the evening, in the garden of Eden. It means living out of a place of complete love and acceptance as they did. Where God directs your life from listening to his voice, from a position of faith and not from our own judgement of what is 'right' and 'wrong'.

So what about this other tree? The tree of the knowledge of good and evil. After eating from this tree the Godhead said that *"**man has now become like one of us**, knowing good and evil"* **(Genesis 3:22).** There was something about this tree that would make Adam and Eve 'like God', but would also take them completely away from the way that God had intended them to live. The tree had fruit that *"was good for food and pleasing to the eye, and also desirable for gaining wisdom"* **(Genesis 3:6),** though probably not apples as described in our Sunday school stories. I can't remember the last apple I ate that gave me more wisdom. What we do know is that the tree and the fruit were somehow attractive and that God especially highlighted this tree to Adam and Eve and warned them that *"you must not eat from the tree"* **(Genesis 2:17)**. This reveals that God was aware of the tree's attractiveness and tempting properties for Adam and Eve. It is a very interesting thought as to why God allowed this tree to be there in the first place? After all, he says in scripture that he does not tempt man. **James 1:13** says that "*...no one should say that, 'God is tempting me'.* **For God cannot be tempted by evil, nor does he tempt anyone."**

God, knowing that Adam and Eve would be at great pains to resist tasting the fruit from the tree of the knowledge of good and evil and the cunningness of Satan himself, plants this tree to be in his garden of perfection. I have always been confused by this because it almost seems outside of the character of God for him to do this.

One night before I was due to teach about The Two Trees at YWAM my wife awoke in the morning having had a very interesting dream. In the dream she had seen Satan planting the tree of the knowledge of good and evil in the Garden of Eden. If this were true, then it was not God's original intention to have this tree in the Garden of Eden but the scheme and work of the enemy himself. After all, it is in his character to tempt and to accuse. In **2 Corinthians 11:14** he is also described as masquerading "as an angel of light." Both trees contain knowledge but the tree of life comes from God and we respond in faith, whilst the tree of knowledge of good and evil is how we ourselves determine right and wrong. The source could not be more different.

Could Satan have planted a tree that imitates the life and direction of God but from a completely different source? I have not been able to prove categorically that this did happen, as scripture does not confirm this. However, I also believe that scripture does not refute this either. God highlights that he made all kinds of trees that were pleasing to the eye and good for food, but he does not make clear whether this included the tree of the knowledge of good and evil.

> **Genesis 2:9**
> *The Lord God made all kinds of trees grow out of the ground—trees that were pleasing to the eye and good for food.* ***In the middle of the garden were the tree of life and the tree of the knowledge of good and evil.***

I don't want to make a doctrine about this and it may be a leap too far to suggest that Satan did indeed plant this tree. But it poses the question as to why God would plant it? Many would suggest this was a test to see if they would obey God. Perhaps it was, but it is hard to imagine God creating a tree that was pleasing to the eye and good for food that Adam and Eve could neither touch nor eat. Why plant a tree that was so good and then say, "by the way, see that tree with the beautiful fruit that is fantastic to eat, leave it alone or you will die." That was a temptation too great to bear for Adam and Eve and to me it almost seems to conflict with God's character and his desire for them to live in the garden with him eternally.

Regardless, the tree was there and God made it very clear that it was something that Adam and Eve should not eat from and they would indeed be tempted to do so. As the story goes, Satan then appears to Adam and Eve. The temptation becomes too great for them and they eat from the fruit of the tree of the knowledge of good and evil. At this time the bible says that ***"the eyes of both of them were opened,*** *and they realised they were naked"* (**Genesis**

3:7). But what "eyes" is this passage referring to when it says that their eyes were opened? We know that their real eyes were already formed and opened. Furthermore, we see the term 'eyes' often used as a metaphor for the heart in scripture. One example is in **Ephesians 1:18**. Here Paul says that "*he prays that **the eyes of your heart may be enlightened in order that you may know the hope to which he has called you…***" In this he describes the heart as metaphorically having eyes. The fact that he prays that they would be enlightened indicates that the eyes of our heart appear to have dimed or closed since the fall. There are many other places where the eyes of the heart are referenced and described metaphorically in scripture, especially when Jesus speaks about the Pharisees' hearts. In **Acts 28:27** Paul says that "their eyes have closed", when speaking of the Pharisees. Again he is clearly not speaking about their actual eyes but about their hearts.

> **Acts 28:27 *(NKJV)***
> *For the **hearts of this people have grown dull. Their ears are hard of hearing, and their eyes they have closed**, Lest they should see with their eyes and hear with their ears, Lest they should understand with their hearts and turn, So that I should heal them.*

Throughout scripture it seems to be the mission of Jesus, Paul and the church to reopen the eyes of people's hearts so that they can again see God as he truly is.

So if anything the eyes of the heart were closed or dimmed at the fall. However, when Adam and Eve eat from the tree of the knowledge of good and evil the scripture says that their 'eyes' are opened. So it must be another set of eyes that are being referred to here.

The bible says that the eyes that were opened made them like God (**Genesis 3:22**), knowing both good and evil. Assumably before this they only knew love and goodness and walking with God was their reference point to good and evil. They had no need for 'eyes' to see what was right and wrong or good and evil. I think we can say that the eyes that opened in the garden were the eyes of the mind to be able to judge 'good' and 'evil' and in this way mankind became 'like God'. This might sound a bit like a reward to 'become like God', but in fact we know it was a consequence of disobedience and it opened their 'eyes' to live in a way that God never intended.

Man could now judge good and evil and could live independently of God, making decisions that were now wise in their own eyes. It also opened their eyes to see what was good, so that they could now do all kinds of good with no connection to faith and hearing God. Self-righteousness and self-assessment could now become the way of assessing how much 'good' and how much 'evil' we do. We had now become 'like God' in being able to judge good and evil, without having to have connection to him or be in submission to his leadership. This one decision opened up the way for mankind to enter into all kinds of beliefs and opinions that they believed to be 'right'. It sounds great except it was not the way that God intended for mankind to live. Since this time, even as Christians, we predominantly live from this tree, assessing every decision others and ourselves make, as either 'good' or 'evil'. Even the wisdom that comes from this tree in regards to doing good can be deceptive. It has opened the way for us to have an opinion on everything and everyone regardless of whether this is connected to God's heart or not. We can now evaluate for ourselves which churches are doing it 'right' and which ones are doing it 'wrong'. Our opinions and judgements can be so strong that there is no need at times to ask

God his thoughts, as 'we already know'.

When we think of eating from the tree of the knowledge of good and evil we often only think of the evil that came out of that decision. But there was also a corrupted good that came from the tree that is totally disconnected from the heart of God. It is a good that does not come from a place of faith or connection with God, but from our own judgements. We can even evaluate our own or others righteousness through the lens of; have I done enough 'good' things and avoided enough 'bad' or 'evil' things? This diverts us from the cross in which we became righteous because of Christ and what he did there. Even as Christians we can move away from the gospel and into a kind of false gospel, trying our hardest to eliminate enough bad and do enough good to become righteous in our eyes and in the eyes of others. We can now judge and evaluate what is good not from a place of faith or hearing God, but from our own opinions and beliefs. Sometimes this way of judging and evaluating has become so ingrained in our nature that we do not even realise we are operating from it. We immediately think that because we evaluate a decision as 'good' or 'evil', it must somehow be from the Lord.

For example, the 'good' from this tree can lead us to focus on creating our own standard of 'good'. This is what led the Pharisees to develop a way of living that may have been 'good' in their own eyes but was far from the heart of the Father's love, compassion and mercy. The Pharisees did not turn away from God's heart by committing acts of evil as we might understand them. They became separated from the love of God by trying to achieve righteousness in their own strength and by doing good that was not connected to God's heart or as we might now understand, from the 'Tree of Life'.

In a way the Pharisees loved rules and being seen by others as 'good', more than they loved God or people. They had forgotten that the law could be summed up in one command, "**Love your neighbour as yourself**" and that "**love is the fulfilment of the law**" (Romans 13:9-10).

In some ways the modern church has fallen into this trap too. I walked into this well intentioned trap in my Christian walk, living predominantly from the tree of the knowledge of good and evil and wondering why I felt distant from the love of God.

As a young Christian I was determined to be the 'best' Christian that I could be. I went to bible college and learnt to discipline myself in the Christian disciplines. I read my bible each morning and sometimes morning, afternoon and night. I prayed as best as I could, "*without ceasing*" (**1 Thessalonians 5:17**), I shared my faith often and I learnt to fast. At bible college I remember reading about John Wesley and the methodist pastors and how they fasted twice a week. I decided that was something I could do. I also did longer fasts – 21 days with only juice and 40 days on a Daniel (restricted food) fast. I set out to do as much good as I could, but the problem is, how much good is good enough for God? When you get stuck in trying to be good, when is it enough?

I had very high standards for myself and others, but this was often not accompanied with love, mercy and compassion for people. I judged myself and others harshly and couldn't even live up to the standards I had set myself. At times I succeeded in being a 'good Christian' in my eyes and at other other times I failed miserably. This caused me to swing between self-righteousness and condemnation in my life. After seven years of being a Christian, attending bible college, getting married, and doing everything I could to serve

CHAPTER 4

God, we got the call to attend Youth with a Mission (YWAM) in the South Island of NZ. The course that we felt to be a part of had a focus on the 'Father's love' and this was also the title of the school. In my head I knew what 'Father's Love' meant and I had some experience of this from reading John Eldridge's book, 'Wild at Heart'. But in all honesty I did not really know the Father at this time and did not live in a true experience of his love.

Prior to leaving for this school we had to pack up the house which was a bit easier in those days as we only had one child. Carolyn and baby left to go down south earlier so she could get ready for her sister's wedding. We would then be staying at Carolyn's parents for about ten weeks in Nelson before the school started in Christchurch. So Carolyn got to fly down and I spent the last few days doing the final clean and packing up our rented house. During this time on my own I spent some time farewelling a few friends, one of whom was a very good friend of mine who was in the leadership team at the Christian school where I worked. I loved hanging out with this guy because he enjoyed talking about the Lord. He had a way of being so encouraging and didn't seem as driven and judgemental as I was. He was always very honest with me but not in a condemning way. So as we sat one afternoon I asked him what he thought about my preaching. I wasn't fishing for a compliment, as in my time of preaching at school and church I had received plenty of compliments affirming this gift in me and yet I sensed something was missing. I would often feel really condemned after I preached. I was actually truly reflecting on this gift and wanting some answers as to why things didn't seem quite at peace within. He began to describe how there is love and truth and that they work in unison. For example, Jesus was always truthful and yet being God in the flesh he always spoke the 'truth in love'. Everything he said was motivated by love because God is love, not just loving, but actually *is* love. My friend Shane suggested that my preaching was very high in 'truth' but not so high in 'love' and if I could ever match God's love with his truth then it would be amazing. My friend said this in complete love and I could not fault anything that he said, as it rang true. It reminded me of Paul's words in **1 Corinthians 13** where he says we can do many things but if they don't come from love they sound like a clanging cymbal. How much of my preaching had sounded like a clanging cymbal? And how much of my life sounded like a clanging cymbal? I could not get this new-found revelation off my mind as I took the two day drive down to Nelson. I reflected on the fact that I had done so many things in my Christian walk, but after seven years I could honestly say that I lacked love for others and that I was judgemental of myself and other Christians. All I had done in my Christian life felt like empty works and, as Paul describes in **Philippians 3:8**, as 'worthless' compared to knowing Christ. I had tried so hard to please God, to be a good Christian and had failed to show the love that Christ did. What could I do now? I was bankrupt.

After we go through a time of pain or longing we often see afterwards that God was setting us up for a healing or a revelation of great significance. In this case, this was exactly what God was doing. We arrived in a small town called Oxford, near Christchurch, surrounded by hills, mountains and green fields. It would be a quiet and pretty place in which to complete the course. We were welcomed with open arms by the staff and other students and quickly realised that we were in a great place of love and acceptance, one that I hadn't experienced quite like this up until this time. It was about the second or third week when speakers came from a ministry called FatherHeart Ministries. Both speakers had a presence around them that spoke of love and acceptance; this is what I longed for. As the week got going I began to find their teaching a little unsettling as they spoke a lot about love and comfort and spoke adoringly about God as their 'Father'. I was upset because they weren't talking about doing lots of prayer, or evangelism or fasting and to me these were the things that were the benchmark of a successful Christian. Then came the kicka – a teaching on the two lost sons from the story in **Luke 15** titled 'The Prodigal Son'. I knew the story well, having been like the younger son in my rebellious teens and twenties and then finding a forgiving heavenly Father when I was 27 years old. So I wasn't expecting to get much from the story, except that they hardly spoke about the younger brother, focusing rather on the older brother. This son had been faithful to the Father's business and had to suffer the indignity of watching his brother leave the family with his inheritance. But new insights came to me this week. The older brother had been slaving away for the Father and had never disobeyed one of his orders, yet he showed very little love for his brother or his Father. He was angry that his Father had never given him anything and yet the Father said that everything he had belonged to the older brother. The older brother sounded more like a slave than a much loved son. Could it be that I was living more like a slave to God than a son to a loving Father?

> **Luke 15: 25-32**
> *Meanwhile, the older son was in the field. When he came near the house, he heard music and dancing. So he called one of the servants and asked him what was going on. 'Your brother has come,' he replied, 'and your father has killed the fattened calf because he has him back safe and sound.'*
> *The older brother became angry and refused to go in.*

> *So his father went out and pleaded with him. But he answered his father,* **'Look! All these years I've been slaving for you and never disobeyed your orders. Yet you never gave me even a young goat so I could celebrate with my friends. But when this son of yours** *who has squandered your property with prostitutes comes home, you kill the fattened calf for him!'*
> *'My son,' the father said, 'you are always with me, and everything I have is yours. But we had to celebrate and be glad, because this brother of yours was dead and is alive again; he was lost and is found.'*

That week of teaching on the Father's Heart broke me in a good way. God began to share with me how after seven years of being a Christian I had become much more like the older brother than the younger brother. I was slaving away for the Father but was harsh on myself and other people. I was all about working hard for the Kingdom but lacked love and mercy. At salvation I had known a good God who showed grace to his children, but now I was serving a hard task master who was predominantly interested in my work. He loved me when I was doing his work but if I was lying on the couch, I wasn't so sure.

I shed many tears during those two weeks, but I also laughed with joy like I had never experienced. I felt bathed in a love that I did not think was possible with God. I went from having my identity as a hard working slave that could never do enough for God to feeling like a loved son. Could it be that the reason I could not show love to others was because I had never allowed myself to be unconditionally loved?

A new journey began that week and I have never been the

CHAPTER 4

same since.

I came into a relationship with God the Father as his beloved son rather than as a hard working slave. I came to relate to God as my 'Abba Father', the way Paul describes God. Even David had this revelation in **Psalm 2:7** when God declared, "You are my son; today I have become your father." Before this I had known that God was 'the Father' and I even prayed to him as such, but after this time I knew him as 'my Father'. He went from just being Jesus' Father, to now being *my* Father. Jesus was my brother, as Jesus was *"the firstborn of many brothers"* that is foretold in **Romans 8:29.** I will add that Jesus is still saviour and Lord but also my dear brother.

This revelation changed the whole way I related to God and enabled me to receive love as a son and not feel like I was always working for love. As this love began to penetrate my life I began to progressively operate less out of condemnation (more on this later). I also found that I was no longer judging myself and others as harshly and could have compassion and mercy on others. I was beginning to live from the 'tree of life' again, from the love of my Father and from listening to his voice, as God had always intended. I had lived from the tree of the knowledge of good and evil for a long time, trying to do enough good and eliminate enough bad in my life to keep God happy. I could never please God in this way. My walk with him needed to begin with the revelation that my life does give God pleasure and that by him living through me I could live a fruitful, loved filled life.

I began to live less from condemnation and less from a viewpoint of 'I have to do this because God is demanding me too'. I began to live more from the prompting of the Spirit and the urgings of faith and I discovered more peace, more love and more satisfaction in my life. The Father was a loving God who wanted me and wanted to work through me. He did not want a slave who could only relate to him in the matter of work. As I lived like this I found I could live more from a perspective of faith. I realised I actually didn't have to have an opinion on anything and everything. And I don't have to have mastery of all scripture and have my theology all locked down and worked out. I can see God's word with a great deal more mystery and be completely ok with this.

When I preach now I am listening for a word of faith and to what the Father is saying to me. Then I share from this place of heart revelation, even if the theology may seem imperfect to some. I know a word of faith has so much more power than me trying to fight to get my point of view across, as this comes from the tree of the knowledge of good and evil. When I preach from faith I can be at complete peace about what I have said, not thinking I have all the answers but being content to be a mouthpiece for a small amount of the revelation God wants to share with people. How much more life-giving and peaceful is this?

Living by faith and out of a place of being loved is what it means to walk metaphorically out of the tree of life. It is how it began for Adam and Eve and I believe to a degree we can continue to walk this way. Our eyes may have been opened to judge 'good' and 'evil', but our true design was not to live out of our imperfect judgements but out of a place of communing and listening to the Father and responding to this. In other words, out of a place of Faith. I continue to see the eyes of my heart enlightened and opened to God. The eyes of judgement that opened in the Garden of Eden have not brought me closer to God's heart and I long to keep coming back to living from the tree of life.

CHAPTER 5
WHEN GOD SAYS NO

When we walk in faith it is important we learn to live with the 'no' as well as the 'yes' of God. When a door closes for us and God is saying no, it can often bring feelings of rejection and hopelessness, especially when we have been believing in something for a long time. But the no of God can open up many doors because as we say no to one door, we allow other doors to open.

After I was offered a job to come to Queensland as a teacher, the Principal rang me up to see if I was interested in taking on a small leadership role as a year group leader. He had only met me on zoom but said that from reading all of my experience on my resume he felt like I would do a good job. Carolyn and I were completely honoured by his request. I had only been back in teaching for a few years after having a break, but I felt trusted and seen by him. I really wanted to take on this little extra challenge and so did Carolyn. But the more I prayed, the more I felt like God was saying that saying yes to this would mean saying no to many other things that I could use my time for. In the end I politely declined the offer but it was very tempting. In hindsight I see that God used me for many other things because I did not have this extra time constraint and I was so glad that I had said no.

Sometimes we continue to push on a door that is closed, when God has already moved on to something else for us and we are missing out on this opportunity. In our orphaness we think that nothing could be as good as what we had envisioned and that God must have forgotten us, rejected us, or given us the crumbs. In **1 Samuel 16** the prophet Samuel is sent by God to anoint the next King. He has his own ideas on who this will be. As he observes Eliab (the oldest son) he thinks that surely this is the Lords anointed **(1 Samuel 16:6)**. But the Lord tells him that he has rejected him and that *"the Lord sees not as man sees: man looks on the outward appearance, but the Lord looks on the heart"* **(v7)**. The Lord continues to reject each of his brothers until Samuel asks if there are any other brothers. Jesse replies that there is still the youngest but that he is tending the sheep **(v11)**. David is brought in simply as an afterthought but Samuel hears the words ***"arise, anoint him, for this is he"*** **(1 Samuel 16:12)**. David is anointed as Israel's next King.

If Samuel had not operated in faith we would not read the story of David and Goliath in the bible or have witnessed a man after God's own heart, one of the greatest Kings of all time. If he had operated out of his natural and logical mind then he would never have heard the no of God and anointed David as King. Faith has different eyes to our natural eyes. If we are not careful we can become people who see things only with our natural eyes and not with our Spirit in faith. In **Isaiah 11** there is a prophecy written about Jesus and it says in **verse 3** that *"he will not judge by what he sees with his eyes or decide by what he hears with his ears"*. In other words Jesus would operate in faith and not in what he sees naturally. He would see with the eyes of his heart and move by the Spirit. Jesus only did what he saw his Father doing and no doubt this meant knowing when his Father was saying no or closing a door. Even the life Jesus lived is not the most logical or maybe what we would do. Jesus only revealed himself as the Messiah and did the Father's work for three years and only remained in Israel. Why not go to the rest of the known world? Why not hang around for 50 years and do millions of miracles that could be undeniable to all men? But Jesus walked in faith, in complete flow with his Father and not with his natural eyes.

When we moved back to Australia a few years ago we had our sights set on a school that was in the North of Brisbane. We had applied for it 18 months before we left NZ, paid our application fees and as far as we were concerned it was a done deal. Carolyn, after initially 'never' wanting to move to Australia, had finally come around to the idea about the possibility and had googled Christian schools north of Brisbane. The first school that came up on the search engine drew her eyes and she felt that it was the school that God had for us. When I saw the school's website I agreed that this school had to be the one. The name of the school was also the same as our youngest child, so as far as we were concerned that was confirmation that we were going to be there. We did not even look at any other schools but put all our eggs in the one basket, believing that this was the school that God had chosen for us. Schools that have waiting lists generally let you know around September the year before if you have been accepted so you can begin to prepare. So we simply waited for September to come but at the same time believed that it was a certain 'yes'. We then received an email in August saying that our children had not been accepted, but we could remain on the waiting list for the following year if we wished. Did we hear God wrong? Was the school not listening to God? Or was this just a first move and we would get in another way?

We weren't that concerned at this stage because we still believed God wanted us to go to this school. I would apply for a job as soon as one became available and once I got accepted the kids would become first priorities and would also be accepted. This was our line of thinking. So when a job came up for a PE and Maths teacher in my year groups, I was certain that this was our way in. I filled out the application and then waited to receive an interview. I wasn't being presumptuous about the job, but I was just so confident in God and in faith that this was what he had for our family. So when the email came back thanking me for my application and letting me know that I would not be receiving an interview, I was confused, a little annoyed and eventually devastated. My first thought was that they had made a mistake and that maybe they were not listening to God in this. I actually nearly rang and said this to the Principal, though I'm glad now that I did not allow my pride to allow such a reaction. We had waited nearly 18 months and had hung our plans on this act of faith and now the door slammed in our face.

I believe that God works through open and shut doors and it is his way of saying yes and no to us. Sometimes we need to knock a few times just to see if this is indeed the Lord, but eventually we need to accept that right now this appears to be a 'no'. After not being given an interview at the school we had pursued and our kids not being accepted we could have continued to see if other jobs were available. We could have waited another year for the possibility of the kids being accepted. That night as I sought the Lord I felt to let go of the dream of going to this school. The door had shut and it would not be reopened. I went to bed that night disappointed and confused but I did feel like the Lord gave me these words: "Wait until tomorrow". There is an expression that we use, "tomorrow is a new day". In God, tomorrow can change everything. In **Psalm 30:5** it says that *"weeping may last a night but the joy comes in the morning"*. God uses days and weeks and years to bring change and to reward our faith. While we may be mourning one day, we may be celebrating with joy the next.

The next day after accepting that the door had closed on our plans and the school, I opened up 'Seek' (a website where all the teaching jobs are advertised). I had checked this site many times prior even though we had not seriously considered applying for other jobs, as we felt that we had our school lined up. But on this occasion a school stood out very clearly to me. It was just 20 minutes North from the other one, was a Christian school and was in the kind of socio-economic area that I had worked in most of my career. I figured I had done up my resume suitably for the other job and that I could almost just drop the same one in and see what happened. So I did that and then I waited in faith. I had faith and hope again, that whilst God had allowed our first dream to die that this could indeed be a resurrection. A week later I received an email asking me for an interview with the school. I took the interview and was accepted just weeks later as were all our kids. Why does God allow us to feel like a dream is dead only to resurrect it in his way? Was he not in the original plan? We had surrendered our plan to him and he did not divert us until the 11th hour.

These are good questions and I'm not always sure of the answer but I believe that God actually finds the journey of faith more important than the result. With God, a good result is a sure thing, but the journey and the detail is always up for debate. I believe God will often take us into the unknown and allow us to be unsure so that we put our trust in him completely. The result is not a matter of following good principles or the best strategy (think of the story of Gideon and Israel). God's reward is the result of following him through all manner of rabbit holes and knowing that there is no way you would have got here without him. You would not have chosen that way and only a loving and maybe a bit of a playful Father would take us on that journey.

Abraham is a great example of faith in God being more important than knowing the way. Abram (as he is called at this point) is called by God to go to a land that he will give him. How exciting this will be, right? The Lord says to Abram *"Go from your country, your people and your father's household to the land I will show you"* **(Genesis 12:1)**. Hang on a minute – leave your country, your family, your friends, your comfort and everything you have ever known and I'm going to show you a country…somewhere. What? Leave behind everything you know for a land you can not see, touch or even have an inkling of where it might be. Abraham knew that God was good and whether he heard the 'yes' or the 'no' of God that he would be led to good things. To have faith you have to trust in the character of God. Faith is the ultimate test as to whether we actually believe in the goodness of God. No one in their right mind will trust someone with the most important details of their lives (homes, future partner, job, where to live etc.) unless they know they have the best in mind for them. Faith is like this with God. You aren't going to follow his word unless you know that he is indeed trustworthy. When you live in faith, God's reputation begins to build in your heart until you begin to know that even if he tells you to give up all you have, you know that he has something good for you in return.

When you value the 'yes' or 'no' of God in your life more than you value your reputation, then you can begin to walk in faith. Early in the book I described a school I had worked at for students with attendance and behavioural difficulties, which was run by Youth off the Streets. I described that it was a challenging and at times uncomfortable period in my life. I was a new Christian with so much zeal and plenty of inexperience in how best to share this. My view was that everybody needed to hear about Jesus and it was my job to let them know. Some of this zeal got knocked around a bit in this job. Whilst the school was affiliated with a church denomination it did not employ people of faith exclusively and so it was a mix of many philosophies. One of these philosophies was that we weren't to pray or share faith with the students. So when I decided to pray for safety before driving on an excursion one day, it didn't come as a surprise that a few days later I received a warning from the Principal. I was not to pray with the students and this was again made clear to me. I also clashed with the boss; God was working on my submission as I had real problems submitting to my female Principal. It didn't help that we only saw her on Fridays as she worked at three different affiliated schools. When she would come in one day a week and tell us what we needed to be doing, I had trouble receiving her advice. In any case, God was teaching me about submission and honour and at this point in my life I struggled with both.

After 12 months of working at this school I was desperate to get out. I really wanted to get back to a conventional classroom and be part of school life with all the camps, carnivals and trips that I enjoyed. When a job came up at a local Catholic school for a PE and Maths teacher with the added bonus of coaching rugby league, I was excited. I applied for the job and was asked to go in for an interview. I told my supervisor and she was understanding and happy for me. I took a morning off to go to my interview and got ready in my suit and tie. I drove to a cafe to prepare for the interview. As I sat down I had a real sinking feeling that I was not supposed to go for this job. That feeling would not leave me and I lost all my peace about it. I just knew I had to ring the school and tell them. So that's what

I did. I rang and told them that I was extremely sorry for the late notice but that I couldn't come to the interview. I hated telling the secretary that I wasn't coming as I was a people pleaser and did not like letting people down, but I was learning to walk with God and respond to his voice. I went back to my school and told my supervisor that I hadn't gone through with the interview. I would finish what I started. The rest of the year had some amazing blessings and things started to turn around for me at that place. Later in the year when I felt the call to go to bible college, which I have described in an early chapter, it confirmed that the 'no' of God had now opened up an amazing 'yes'. I was so excited with where God was leading me and I couldn't help but thank God for his leading.

We must see God's leading from the tree of life and not get caught in trying to see decisions from the tree of the knowledge of good and evil. Sometimes it can be a good thing that God says 'no' to. We ask ourselves how something so good could not be in the plans of God. When Paul was on his ministry journey he was prevented from entering Asia by the Holy Spirit. We are not told why and it's a fair chance Paul wasn't either, he just knew the door was shut and there was no way of entering.

> **Acts 16:6**
> *Paul and his companions travelled throughout the region of Phrygia and Galatia,* **having been kept by the Holy Spirit from preaching the word in the province of Asia.**

At times our plans may be very good yet we are not called to walk in 'good plans', but in faith.

Faith requires us to keep in step with the Spirit and know that the doors God opens will close others and the doors he closes will open others. When we learn to trust in his leadership we can know that his plans are indeed good, pleasing and perfect **(Romans 12:2)**, even if they don't always 'make sense' right now.

CHAPTER 6
REVELATION & CONDEMNATION

If we are to walk in faith we must learn to live from a place of revelation. When we receive revelation we can now see something that we did not see before. It is what we might call an 'ah-huh' moment where all of a sudden we see something that was hidden to us previously. We might have read a scripture passage 100 times but one day the Holy Spirit shines his light on it and all of sudden God reveals something to our hearts. Revelation and knowledge are two different things entirely. We can know lots of things about something and study the subject, but revelation is when the Holy Spirit shines light on something that gives us a heart understanding. For example we might know lots of scripture passages about love, but we may not have a revelation of God's love for us. When it comes it goes deep into our heart and begins to change us from within. Revelation will bring deep changes in our life and in our understanding of God, ourselves and others.

Peter received the revelation that Jesus was *"the Christ, the Son of the Living God"* in **Matthew 16:16**. Jesus goes on to say that *"this was not revealed to you by man, but by my Father in heaven"* **(v17)**. In other words, Peter did not receive this revelation from studying a text or listening to others. This was revealed to him by the Holy Spirit and its origin was from the Father. There is no doubt that this moment changed his life and no amount of study or debate would change this revelation. When we experience revelation it becomes cemented in our hearts and a foundation of who we are in Christ.

When I went to Faith Bible College in NZ I received the gifts of the Holy Spirit. Speaking in other tongues, the gift of prophecy, the gift of faith, and the gift of healing, to name a few. I began to use these in my life and walk in them. I have since always been involved in multi-denominational Christian organisations and I love the variety of people that you meet in those. Occasionally I will meet someone who's belief is that speaking in tongues has now ceased or that some of the other gifts are no longer active. I can respect this point of view but because I have had a revelation of these gifts, I can no longer deny there reality in my life any more than I can deny the nose on my face. Revelation causes us to have a deep assurity in some area of God so that we will stand on this understanding no matter what.

When we get revelation it means we can walk in faith because we have an understanding of what God is saying and we stand firm in that. In a way, before revelation comes, we are walking in ignorance in an area of our life where we cannot walk in faith. This ignorance is not intentional and it may not even be sinful, but just a product of not receiving revelation from God in that area.

When I was teaching at Bethlehem College in NZ I used to teach Christian Living, a subject I enjoyed very much. As one of my gifts is preaching, at times I would preach or teach rather than giving the class student centred activities. If I was unorganised or not prepared enough for the class I was more likely to actually revert to just talking to the students. One night at parent teacher interviews this blind spot was revealed to me by a 12 year old girl and her dad. Parent teacher interviews were always interesting for teachers because some teachers would become quite nervous if something negative was said about them or their practices questioned. In my experience the majority of feedback you received from parents was positive, but occasionally you would receive some negative feedback and I found this became an opportunity to reflect on that area of teaching and consider whether I needed to change. At this school the students would nearly always come with their parents and I would always ask them if they had any questions or concerns. On this occasion I had a fairly quiet and respectful girl in front of me with her Dad. I gave a report back about her behaviour and grades and then asked if she wanted to say something. The young girl looked back and forth to her father several times before he spoke up for her. "There is just one thing," he said. "When you are teaching Christian Living she says you are talking too much and it is ruining it for the kids." I was taken aback by the statement but it was said with complete respect and it did not come across as criticism. I thanked the Dad and student for the feedback and finished the rest of my interviews. Later that night as I was driving home I was able to reflect on what they had said. I could see that I had turned Christian Living into a subject where I talked and they listened. The students needed to be able to explore God for themselves, discuss things, share their views and use other teaching and learning methods. I had missed the mark and I knew it. I came back to school and changed the way I taught Christian Living, giving the students much more input and student centred activities. This changed the class and the Holy Spirit was able to flow again.

This revelation changed the way I saw things and enabled me to make a change. This is what happens when we receive revelation from God. We have that 'ah-huh' moment and it causes change that supersedes our knowledge on a subject.

One of the greatest enemies of revelation and faith is condemnation. When we feel that we are under God's disapproval it becomes difficult for us to walk in faith and believe that God may actually have good things for us. When I say that condemnation is God's disapproval of us, what I mean is that's what it feels like. We believe the voice of condemnation to be God, when it is really the enemy or our own voice speaking into our hearts. This voice is speaking so loudly to us that it blocks out the voice of God and what he might be saying. I used to think that condemnation was a good thing and I would often think that the voice of condemnation was God. I thought that punishing myself was a very religious and Godly thing to do. Condemnation and self punishment actually take us away from the gospel (good news). The gospel is that Jesus came to take our punishment for us and take away sin and its harmful effects. When we hold onto sin and feel like we should be punished for it (after we know what Jesus has done for us), we limit the power of the cross and actually turn away from what Jesus did. We try to take that sin on ourselves. We become very focused on our sin, something that has already been dealt with. To walk in freedom and from a place of revelation we first have to get rid of condemnation. Many people will try and get free of their sin but are caught up in condemnation. They then wonder why they keep sinning, but in my experience condemnation always drives us back to sin.

The diagram above shows us how the condemnation cycle works. When we sin we feel condemned and shamed. At this point in the cycle we need to go to Christ and get rid of condemnation. To remind ourselves that there is "*now no condemnation for those who are in Christ Jesus*" (**Romans 8:1**). But for many of us condemnation

```
        FAILURE and
           SIN
   ↗              ↘
SELF PUNISHMENT/
  WORK HARDER        SHAME and
    (The Law)       CONDEMNATION
           ↖      ↙
```

drives us to self-punishment or back to the works of the law. We might say 'because I have sinned I am going to make it up to God and I'm going to read the bible more, pray more and worship more.' We set ourselves more rules so that we can establish our own kind of righteousness, inadvertently taking us away from the true gospel. If we have any sense of will power we might even stick to these rules for a while and feel like we are succeeding as a Christian again. We are climbing the totem pole of Christianity and doing well. At this point we might experience some self-righteousness due to our good works. However, in the end what goes up must come down and due to some kind of crisis or illness or tough time in our life, we break our rules again and go sliding down the totem pole. We have failed again and go back to condemnation and shame. If we have the strength we might go back to this cycle again or in some extreme cases we might just give up trying to follow Christ because it's just too hard. This reflects a movement away from the true gospel.

My friend and author Stephen Hill demonstrates this point using the story of the women caught in adultery.

> **John 8:3-11**
>
> *The teachers of the law and the Pharisees brought in a woman caught in adultery. They made her stand before the group and said to Jesus, "Teacher, this woman was caught in the act of adultery. In the Law Moses commanded us to stone such women. Now what do you say?" They were using this question as a trap, in order to have a basis for accusing him.*
>
> *But Jesus bent down and started to write on the ground with his finger. When they kept on questioning him, he straightened up and said to them, "Let any one of you who is without sin be the first to throw a stone at her." Again he stooped down and wrote on the ground.*
>
> *At this, those who heard began to go away one at a time, the older ones first, until only Jesus was left, with the woman still standing there. Jesus straightened up and asked her, "Woman, where are they?* **Has no one condemned you?"**
>
> *"No one, sir," she said.*
>
> **"Then neither do I condemn you,"** *Jesus declared.* **"Go now and leave your life of sin."**

John shows how Jesus first takes away his disapproval of her (condemnation) and then deals with the sin issue. He first says that he does not condemn her and then tells her to go sin no more. When this lady, caught in the act of sin, is freed from Jesus' disapproval she is now free to walk away from sin. She may not actually choose to do this, but when condemnation is gone we can now walk in faith and revelation and walk according to the Spirit. This is the way of faith. To walk according to God's voice and not according to the voice of condemnation.

Condemnation will always drive you away from God. Sin doesn't need to drive us away from God and our guilt can actually draw us to him. Think of Peter and Judas. Judas sold out Jesus for thirty pieces of silver to the leaders of the Jewish church. Peter denied Jesus, not just once but three times. Both men sinned against God and both men actually felt deep regret for what they did. Many people regret what they do but it only leaves them with pain and condemnation. Judas knew what he had done to Jesus was wrong but he did not turn back to him for forgiveness, rather allowing his pain to lead him to take his own life. Condemnation can never lead you away from sin but it will always lead you back to sin. Peter on the other hand let his regret turn him towards God and seek forgiveness; we call it repentance. He could have let condemnation take him out. He could have thought, 'I am a bad person, I have sinned against God and I deserve to be punished. In fact I am not worthy of Jesus so I am going to keep my distance from him.' But he turned back like the prodigal son. He was accepted as a son, as was the Prodigal and did not lose his value or his place in the Father's house because of sin. This is the gospel, the good news, that we can turn back to God and find our place back in our favourite chair again in our Father's house. He does not ask us to grovel and work our way back into his favour. That is condemnation and that always keeps us distant from God.

A friend of mine was telling me recently that when he was a new Christian he was full of zeal and loved spending time with God. As time went on he allowed cynicism and the battles of life to draw him away from the kind of relationship he once had. What he said next surprised me. He said that he thought he was disqualified from the calling he once had and at times even questioned his salvation. As I listened to him I couldn't help but think that it was condemnation and not his sin that was keeping him from the relationship he desired with God. His sin had been forgiven and taken away on the cross of Christ but condemnation still held him captive. Condemnation will always try and block out the revelation of God's voice that allows us to walk in faith and from glory to glory. Is it sin disqualifying you from God's calling and the relationship you desire or is it condemnation? Remove the voice of God's disapproval from your life first and then go and "sin no more".

Another statement my friend Stephen Hill makes may at first sound a little radical. He says, "We do deserve the love of God." Let that sink in for a moment. "We do deserve the love of God." Now I know what you might be thinking, we all have fallen short of God's glory and we have all sinned and continue to, so how can we deserve the love of God? If you base the love of God on behaviour, then there isn't one person outside of Christ who deserves the love of the Father. However, we need to consider God's love in a positional sense, that we are his children and children do deserve their parents' love. Not based on their behaviour but on the fact that they are their children and there is a natural love that pours down from adult to child. I have six children and all of them can behave badly at times, but I have never gone to bed at night thinking that I do not love my children because they were bad. I might be disappointed in their behaviour yet they still deserve my undisputed love because I am their Dad. So how much more does our Heavenly Father love us despite the fact that our behaviour doesn't warrant this love? His love is not in question and as his children, of course we deserve his love. When we see God as our Father and we relate to him as his children we are less likely to go down the track of condemnation and think, "I don't deserve love." We can then accept the gospel as it was supposed to be, as 'good news'. We can have our relationship with the Father fully restored because of what Jesus did for us and not live like a slave trying to pay him back for all he has done. When you are free from condemnation you can truly live from a place of revelation and faith. You can hear the Father's voice and make that your gauge for life. Like Paul you can live without even judgement of yourself **(1 Corinthians 4:3)** because you are listening to the Father and his heart.

Prior to being a Christian I was a weekend drinker and I can't remember too many Saturday nights when I didn't get drunk. When I became a Christian the desire for this lifestyle changed immediately. Whilst I was still involved in some of the same groups, I began to drive to events, maybe have dinner and a drink, then go home nice and early. It was a lovely change after years of late nights. For example, I played in an Aussie Rules (AFL) team in Sydney and there was a large drinking culture there, but I felt fine to go out after a game without the need to drink. I really enjoyed the opportunities I got to share my new found faith with my teammates. I even got to see one of my teammates come to faith in Christ after we had several conversations about God. Another teammate who I had a conversation with actually told me he had no need for God and that he was living a 'better' life than most Christians already. So I was surprised to find that, when I saw him a few years later, he had become a man of the Christian faith. He wanted to let me know that our conversations had gotten through.

So it was strange when I was driving down to my friend's

wedding in Wollongong, that I had the thought that maybe I could get drunk tonight. I had been a Christian about six months and obviously still had some of the old desires at work in me. None of my Christian friends would be there and I would be staying walking distance away in the local hostel. I couldn't get my mind away from this line of thinking and when the reception began after the wedding ceremony I found myself taking a drink every time the tray went past. Before I knew it I was drunk. That night I did some really stupid things and when I woke up in the morning I had huge regrets over what I had done. I couldn't shake my feelings of regret and condemnation the next morning. I had a sense that there was no coming back from what I had done. Surely after all the grace and forgiveness I had experienced, I could not be forgiven for going back to my old life. I felt so unworthy that morning and completely separated from Christ. I picked up my bible from the floor of the hostel in desperation and opened it to Hebrews 4. I began to read the words and revelation came to my heart.

> **Hebrews 4:16-17**
> *For **we do not have a high priest who is unable to empathise** with our weaknesses, but we have **one who has been tempted in every way**, just as we are—yet he did not sin. **Let us then approach God's throne of grace with confidence, so that we may receive mercy and find grace to help us in our time of need.***

God had never sinned but he did understand my temptation. If I could turn my face towards his and approach him I could receive his mercy and find grace in my time of need. If I asked for it and accepted it, I was forgiven totally.

I could not believe what I had just read and it took away the condemnation and shame I was feeling. As I drove home that morning I couldn't believe it. Not just that I was forgiven, but that my sin had been totally taken away. I kept thinking of ways that I could pay God back. I began to think of reading the bible more, praying more etc. Basically creating more rules that I would follow to show God that I was truly sorry. God's quiet voice spoke to me that morning saying, "There is now no condemnation for those in Christ Jesus." He didn't want me to work my way back into his favour as I was already in it. Now that I was free of God's disapproval I could get free of my sin. This was about 17 years ago and I have not been drunk since. I was free of condemnation and that allowed me to get free of my sin.

When we get free of condemnation we can be free to walk in God's revelation and be led by his voice. Condemnation is the opposite of faith. It is a voice of punishment and sin management. The gospel allows us to walk freely as his children and listen to his voice each day. When he does convict us of sin it is not to drive us away but to bring us closer to him. How wonderful is this?

When we learn to live more from the voice of revelation and faith we can experience more freedom and life. Many of us have lived listening to condemnation for so long that we often believe it to be God. We need to remember that the accuser of the believers is not God but Satan himself **(Revelation 12:10)**. The voice of accusation is not God, even when what he says is true. God is not an accuser and never will be.

When we lived in Tauranga, NZ, Carolyn and I volunteered for an organisation called Drug Arm and would go out on the streets in a van on Friday and Saturday nights. There were seven teams so we would go out about once or sometimes twice a month. We would carry around a whole heap of bakery food that had been donated to us. We would stop anywhere around the city and give people free food, offer prayer and share the good news about Jesus with people. The leader of our team was an amazing evangelist who spoke with such truth and love and very rarely missed the mark. He had a way of knowing when to take someone deeper into a conversation and when to stop and leave a positive affirmation. He would always ask to pray for people and I can very rarely remember anyone knocking back that prayer. Sometimes he would also speak words of encouragement and prophecy (words of hope and encouragement for the future over someone's life), surprising people with the idea that God could know them. For example, I can remember him asking a young man if he had a music gift, affirming that God had given him this and that one day he would use it for him. The young man who wasn't a Christian left affirmed and encouraged.

One night when our leader could not be there, Carolyn and I were asked to lead the team. We would essentially drive around and ask if anyone felt like going anywhere particular that night. After praying, Carolyn said she felt we should go to Otumoetai. This was a suburb that we rarely went to, as it was basically a residential area. We were much more likely to go to The Strand, an area in Tauranga where the pubs and cafes were, or around the beach where young people congregated. I kept the idea in mind and continued driving. Pretty soon we saw a group of young people alongside the road and pulled up to offer them some food. The van had been going around the streets for many years at this point and was trusted as a 'safe place' for many young people. After giving them some food we asked where they were going? They said they were going to a party at Otumoetai. Now this was a good ten kilometres away and they were walking, so this was strange.

"Would you like a lift?" we said.

"Sure thing," they replied.

It seemed like Carolyn's thought about going to Otumoetai was going to come true after all.

Upon arriving in Otumoetai we could see that there was either one large party or a couple of parties happening, as young people were walking around the streets. We dropped off our new found friends and turned the corner to see a large house party with a few people congregating on the front lawn. We weren't against stopping at parties but it came with a degree of risk and the possibility that we would not be welcomed. On this occasion, with just a few young people out the front, we asked if anyone wanted something to eat. They replied affirmatively and we pulled up. As we got out with the food a positive atmosphere developed between us and the young people. It was obvious that some good conversations were happening, despite the fact many of them were drinking. As we continued to chat more people began to spill out onto the front lawn until about 50 people were gathered there. After some time I was beginning to pack up to leave when I felt that small voice inside of me say, "Tell them about me." It seemed impossible that God would ask me to share about him in front of fifty, 16-18 year old people. However the voice sounded like God so I went and told my wife. Her reply was basically, "Then hurry up and do it." The straight answer was what I needed. So I stopped and said something like, "Everybody, I need your attention for a moment." As you can imagine, the attention of 50 people who have been drinking is not an easy thing to get. At this moment one young man in the crowd started shouting out "Speech! Speech! Speech!" and the crowd of young people fell silent and gathered around me.

CHAPTER 6

I said, "Guys tonight is more than just pies and sausage rolls. It is also about telling you some good news. This news is that God loves you so much that he has given his only son for you and if you believe in him you will have eternal life."

I was basically paraphrasing **John 3:16**. The crowd stood stunned and silent. You could tangibly feel the Holy Spirit at work in the group. The same young man who had got the crowd's attention before started chanting, "Jesus, Jesus, Jesus." The rest of the crowd then joined in until they were all chanting the same thing. I could never have imagined a party full of teenagers chanting the name of Jesus at the top of their voices. It was an incredible and yet humorous moment, when I look back on it. We then went back to packing up and a young man approached me at the back of the van. I could see that he was touched by what had happened and I said, "You have been waiting for those words haven't you?" Using a few colourful words of his own, he acknowledged that this was the case. I prayed with him and he received my words with such an open heart to God. Who knows what God later did in this young man's life but in this moment his heart was totally moved by the Holy Spirit. We moved on with great joy in our hearts after this encounter.

I wish I could say that this encounter had only a positive effect on my life but it led me into a great deal of condemnation. Not long after this night I was at a training day for teachers from a variety of other schools. Instead of being able to relax and enjoy the day with these people, I could not get the nagging thought out of my head that I should be sharing about Jesus with them. I kept thinking back to the night in the van where Jesus had said, "Tell them about me." I could hear those words again but in a completely different tone. The words were accompanied with guilt and condemnation and they also came with the fear to speak them. These words hung around with me for many months after this as I thought I had to share about Jesus with every person I met. I could not relax around people because this was going on inside my head.

One day whilst visiting my parents back in Sydney I decided to go into the city and share with people about Jesus. I had never really shared this way before, but I was still dealing with all the condemnation and guilt and felt like this was now my duty. I had always loved sharing with people about Jesus but it was always in the context of a relationship and had flowed with the conversation and God's leading. Now I was trying to set the beat of the music and I was not enjoying it. That day I shared with a homeless man and prayed for him as well as sharing some money, but overall I just walked around feeling like I was responsible for everyone. Finally, I saw a group of young skateboarders. This is who I would share the good news with. I sat down and watched them skate for a while, waiting for my time to stand up and share with them just like I had at the party. A few times I got up to speak but fear kicked in, so eventually I would sit down again. After doing this for maybe an hour, I thought maybe I needed some more prayer power, so I went away to walk and pray for about half an hour. I went back determined to share with the skateboarders. Again, I got ready to stand up and share and fear kicked in. After another half an hour and several more attempts to stand up and face the skateboarders, I realised that I was driven by fear and this was not going to happen. I despondently walked towards the train station, my head down and condemning thoughts filling my mind. I had let God down. I was a failure and was not fit to be an evangelist for God anymore. I boarded the train and just felt an enormous amount of shame wash over me. As I sat there apologising to God for my failure he began to speak to me in a voice that could only be him.

Essentially, his message was that I was now trying to do this alone. I was trying to do things that God had not asked me to do and had not given me grace to do. I was failing because this was not coming from faith and the initiative of the Father but from my weak flesh. Of course I was unable to be bold and share with people. Any boldness I had before had come from God and a place of faith. He had empowered me and helped me share with people. I now realised that I had been listening to the voice of condemnation ever since that night at the party. I thought it was me who had done this great thing and now I was walking in God's disapproval because I had failed to do it again. I returned to the Father as a son that night and not as a slave anymore. I could never work my way into God's favour, I already had his favour. I could rest and relax in his presence and around other people. I could let conversations flow and I was not responsible for everyone I knew or saw. I was responsible to do and say what my Father was saying to me. I could walk at his pace and not with fear and condemnation. This was a huge moment in my life and it helped me relax, knowing that I was to walk from revelation and faith and not from guilt and fear. What a difference this makes. The voice of condemnation may say the same words as God but it will always be in a completely different tone and it will come with fear. It will come in a driven way where you feel like you have to do something to keep God happy.

Without revelation you can not have faith. We can not walk by faith **(2 Corinthians 5:7)** unless we hear the voice of God. Remember, *"faith comes by hearing, and hearing by the word of God"* (**Romans 10:17**). The greatest enemy to us hearing God and walking in faith will be condemnation. This is when we feel God's disapproval and can not get out from under the weight of our sin despite this now being on Christ. To walk by faith we need to first get free of condemnation and then we will be free to get rid of *"the sin that so easily entangles"* **(Hebrews 12:1).**

CHAPTER 7
FAITH & FINANCE

You couldn't write a book on faith without including a chapter on finances and faith. There is no greater area where faith is expressed than through finances. We live in a world where we are in a tension of being in the Kingdom of God and living in faith while also being under the economic forces of capitalism, where profit and ownership are the motivation for work and business. Many people almost assume that capitalism is God's way. Let me tell you that capitalism is the best economic method we have for living in a fallen world. Many have tried other ways but they have not worked because we live in a sinful, fallen world. However, capitalism is not the Kingdom of God, although God certainly uses it. When we finally get to be with God everyone will be blessed. There will be no believer in lack. There will be no one who can say that they have worked the hardest and therefore deserve more than others. Whilst this type of attitude exists, people will be influenced more by capitalism than faith and the Kingdom of God. In the book of Acts when the first Christian believers were growing, they shared everything in common. The love of God was so evident in them that they wanted to ensure that everyone was blessed and no one was living in lack. **Acts 4:32** says that *"those who believed were of one heart and soul, and* ***no one said that any of the things that belonged to him was his own, but they had everything in common.****"*

There was such a Spirit of love amongst them that they did not want to have ownership of anything but considered that all things belonged to everyone. People were living in complete faith selling their houses and properties and giving the proceeds to the apostles to be distributed amongst the group. Due to this, there was not a needy person among them.

> **Acts 4:34-35**
> *There was **not a needy person among them**, for as many as were **owners of lands or houses sold them** and brought the proceeds of what was sold and laid it at the apostles' feet, and it was **distributed to each as any had need.***

The way the first church was living was very much the way heaven is. Jesus said that *"my kingdom come on earth as it is in heaven"* **(Matthew 6:10).** Many people would suggest that this is how the church should live now. Whilst I agree in principle, it would take a powerful act of faith and would have to be inspired by the love of the Father acting powerfully in people's lives. It would almost have to be in a revival-type atmosphere for us (the church) to ever desire to truly let go of personal possessions and ensure there is not one needy in the church.

Giving in the New Testament is about faith and not obligation. Many people, and I was one of them, were taught to give more out of fear than faith. We have been taught from **Malachi 3** that if we do not bring *"our whole tithe into the storehouse"* **(v10)** we will receive a curse and if we do bring our tithe we will be blessed. Whilst I do believe in first fruits giving (setting aside a part of our income for giving), I do not believe that we have a legal agreement with God anymore to do this. Giving under this legal agreement was all about blessings and curses according to obeying the law but under the new covenant we give as an act of faith and love. In **Hebrews 9:7** the writer says we should "***give what you have decided in your heart to give, not reluctantly*** *or* ***under compulsion,*** for God loves a cheerful giver". In other words we give out of a motive of faith and what we feel God is asking us to do. We do not give out of pressure or suggestion and definitely not from a place of fear that says 'if I don't give, God will not take care of me'.

Giving in the New Testament comes from generosity and love but there is still a return. **2 Corinthians 9:6-11** says that "***whoever sows sparingly will also reap sparingly,*** *and* ***whoever sows generously will also reap generously***". Let me explain this by the example of a vegetable garden. If I were planting tomatoes and I sowed a single seed into my garden I could only expect one tomato plant in return. Now because I only have one seed, maybe I am happy with one tomato plant and next year perhaps I'll plant two or three. But if I plant hundreds of seeds then I am hoping that I will have a return of hundreds of tomato plants. Seeing as I reaped so many tomatoes, maybe I will be able to give away many of my tomatoes and will plant even more next year. Both of these acts of sowing and reaping could be legitimate expressions of faith, according to the seed that each person has. One is not necessarily more blessed by God, but the return is simply a harvest of what was sown.

Giving is not about blessings and curses that come from obeying the law, but rather about sowing and reaping according to faith. For someone to give a very small amount may be a very legitimate act of faith. Their giving may have been inspired by God even though the seed was very small. The widow's offering in **Luke 21** is an example of this, as she gives a very small gift and yet this is an act of faith. Jesus tells the crowd that she has given *"out of her poverty"* whilst others have given *"out of their abundance"* **(v.4)**. He commends her faith over these larger gifts. Likewise, someone could give a very large gift but not from a place of faith. This could come from fear, guilt or even to be seen as generous. The gift that God accepts is by faith and is not based on a legal agreement or obligation.

I do not use the word tithe anymore because it indicates a legal transaction between you and God in which you give under compulsion. Many people give from fear and obligation, believing that if they don't, God has a mark book out keeping track and he will stop providing for them. God wants a people who give according to faith, according to what God is asking us to give and as an expression of love. I will add here that many people 'tithe' as an expression of faith and love. But when people are free in our churches to give under a new covenant approach, freely and from what they have decided in their hearts to give, there is so much more joy in giving. Teaching people to give out of a sense of guilt and necessity may fill up the church accounts but it will never produce in people the kind of freedom that God intended. People can be free to plant one tomato seed or free to plant thousands and if this is done with faith, they can experience God's increase and blessing in accordance with their ability to give. In **2 Corinthians 9:8** it says that "God is able to **bless you abundantly,** so that in all things at all times, having all that you need, **you will abound in every good work.**"

What a promise – that you might abound (exist in a plentiful supply) at all times, having all that you need, for every good work. Put that on your wall as a proclamation. This is a mighty promise to know that when we sow according to faith we can be assured he will provide for us in increasing measure.

While working for YWAM we did not receive a weekly wage but

had to trust God that he would provide for us in other ways. During this season of about eight years my family and I lived in a unique expression of faith and provision. I say it is unique because, as I have already said earlier in the book, we are all called "to live by faith" **(2 Corinthians 5:7)**. Often when a missionary or Christian worker does not live from a wage or set income, we say they are living by faith. This is not really true because all Christians are called to live by faith. When we speak of living in faith in the matter of finances we are really referring to a **belief and trust that God will provide for all of our needs despite any evidence to the contrary.** Whether I earn an income or live trusting God to provide in other ways I am believing that God will take care of my every need and even provide more seed to invest into the lives of others. **2 Corinthians 9:10** says that *"he who **supplies seed to the sower and bread for food** will **also supply and increase your store of seed and will enlarge the harvest** of your righteousness."*

A person may earn an income that enables them to live well beyond their needs, but they can also live in a way that requires them to believe and trust in God's provision. A person can sow into the lives of others around them in such a way that they need to continue to trust God for their seed.

When we did live without a regular income or even an income that met all of our basic needs, it did open up the door for God to provide in very unique ways. When we first started to live this way we did not have a group of regular supporters who put money into our bank account every week or month, so God literally had to provide for us in miraculous ways. Living without an income does not happen because you want to depend on others- trust me, that has never crossed my mind. When we lived without a regular income I tried to make sure I never saw people or a person as my source of supply. However, the most common way that God used to supply our needs was through other people. My trust needed to be focused on God and him providing for us in the way that he had determined. I learnt this when we first got called to go to YWAM as students. The school we would attend would last six months in which we would receive no income and whilst we had money saved up, we would need some monthly support to help us. I went to our church at the time to ask them if they would support us for the next six months while we completed the school. They came back and said they would like to give us $50 a month to help us. I must admit I was a little taken aback. In my mind I expected that they would perhaps give us more and I couldn't help thinking about the money we had 'given' to the church. It was a bad attitude, I know, but it came from a presumption that the church should provide for us. God spoke clearly to me about this – 'I am your provider, I will make sure you have enough.' Our Sunday church was not how God primarily provided for us but he did use many others in the wider church to do so in those six months. It taught me never to look to people for your provision. God is our provider. I am very grateful for the money that the church gave us but God taught me that he will decide where our income comes from.

To talk about our provision during our time working as unpaid volunteers, I need to set a background as to how we came to live in this way. After we finished our school at Youth with a Mission (YWAM) in Oxford NZ, I began to be a relief teacher in several local schools. The predominant school was Oxford School in the town where we lived. During my time there I actually developed a real burden for the students. In a day and age where every kind of philosophy and lifestyle was being thrown at the students, they weren't hearing that they had a God who loved them and wanted to reconcile with them through the cross. This began to break my heart, but also opened up the door for many conversations in the school. I later found out that God had much more for me to do in that place.

One morning I was at church when I had a very strong urge in my Spirit to share my burden for the students and the school. When the opportunity came that morning I came to the front and shared how much my heart was breaking for the young people in the school who did not know they were loved and could have a relationship with their creator. What I said was quite simple. Then I just prayed for the students and the school. After I finished, the church actually gave me a very loud ovation. The ovation was not for me or anything great that I had said but it was an acknowledgement that this was God's heart for the school too. I went back to my seat and thought nothing more of it. After the service I was approached firstly by the Pastor and then by the Youth Pastor. Both of them felt like I was the perfect fit to start a program called 24-7 YouthWork in the school. This was a national youth work program that had started in Christchurch, in which schools would come into a partnership with the local church and community and allow Christian youth workers to come into their schools. I later learned that in a time where the Bible in Schools program (Christian religious instruction) was being eliminated from many schools, Christian youth workers were actually in great demand in many NZ schools. This was occuring because existing schools in the program had experienced great success with the youth workers and the word was getting around.

I went home after church with no desire to be a youth worker in the local school. For one, I knew my income would be almost a third of what my current hourly rate was and my experience with the Youth off the Streets school had discouraged me from doing something like this again. However, out of interest I did look at their website to see what it was. Surely God would not be calling me to Youth Work? I was a teacher after all.

Yet as I began to look into it, I realised that God was saying, 'Yes, I want you to start 24-7 YouthWork in the school.' So after much discussion, 24/7 Youthwork began as a one term trial in Oxford School. The hours were to be between 10 and 15 per week, so it wasn't anywhere near a full time commitment, and the income was to come from the school, the local church, and the community. The activities the youth worker could do in the school could be a unique expression of the school's needs and although it did not involve any kind of Christian teaching, we were free to invite kids to church and youth events. One of the first roadblocks I faced was money. I felt that if I was going to work as a youth worker then with my experience I should at least be on the top hourly rate. At this point we had no community income so it was all on the church and the school. When we started to discuss money it felt like this was going to be a roadblock for the program starting, so I approached the school and my Pastor and said that I would like to start the program for free. I will add I didn't do this flippantly, considering I had a family to support, but it was what I felt God was saying. The program was to begin with an act of faith. They were ok with this but both said they would like to give me some money anyway. At this time I also decided to give up doing relief teaching in the school because I realised that I could not be a teacher and a youth worker in the same school. So my income sources dropped significantly, even though I had a few other schools who would employ me as a

CHAPTER 7

relief teacher from time to time. How would we live now?

Over the next months I saw how God rewards our faith. Almost immediately after starting the program, a friend turned up on our doorstep with an envelope containing $500. Another guy from church wanted to give me a large tray of eggs each week and another supplied me with firewood for the whole winter. The school paid me and so did the church and I could still pick up some relief teaching days when I wasn't doing youth work. The youth work was an amazing opportunity but there was no track to follow and I was essentially making up the activities and program as I went along, which was a blessing and a challenge. I can remember my first day of youth work; I really wanted to start with a bang and do a fun lunchtime activity. As the day got closer I couldn't settle on what I was going to do. I had been given time at the school assembly on my first day at Oxford School to announce and launch the program. When the day finally came it was very windy and the only thing that came to mind was to pick up rubbish at the school during lunchtime and invite students to help me, with chocolate rewards of course. It wasn't the bang I was looking for, but I could see that starting with an act of service was a positive start. After this time I did get to run lot's of fun lunchtime activities but on the first day it felt like this was God's choice to start with a rubbish pick up.

24-7 YouthWork was going fine and establishing itself in the school but I still couldn't really see why God had kept us in the town. I was still helping at YWAM on a part time basis and had been involved in several Father's Love DTS (Discipleship Training Schools), but I felt a lack of purpose. I wasn't getting a lot of relief teaching and so I found myself walking the streets with our two small children in a pram a lot in those days. It was a wilderness type of feeling, wandering the streets, talking with God and wondering, "What am I doing here?" One of the ways my wife likes to hear from God is through doing collages and occasionally we would do these together. It was essentially cutting out pictures and words from magazines that you felt were inspired by God. On this occasion, all the words that kept coming up for me were about leading and leadership. We felt like God was talking to us. However, after coming into a revelation of being a son to God and being content with this, I had promised myself I would not be pursuing leadership opportunities again and that if God wanted me to lead anything he would need to let me know. Not long after this we got a call from the current YWAM leader and one of the elders asked, "Can we come over for a chat?" It's funny when people ask for a chat, so often our mind wanders to the worst possible scenario. Somehow, I thought there had been a dispute and they were asking me to sit in on it. I have no idea how I came to that conclusion. What they did want to ask us was entirely different – "Would we become the new team leaders of YWAM, Oxford?" Now because God had already been speaking to Carolyn and I about leadership in those weeks prior, it was a pretty easy decision to make. So we became the new team leaders of YWAM Oxford. There was no income for this role, so it would again mean trusting God for finances.

So a new season of life started. I was still working as a youth worker in the local school but we had managed to attract two new youth workers. The story of that miraculous provision is for another time. Nevertheless, it meant I could pull back on the hours I was working at Oxford School and spend more time at the YWAM base. So back to finances and faith. We had lived in several different houses since being students at the YWAM base and we now had a small cottage that we really enjoyed opposite YWAM. One day the owner dropped by to say we had six weeks to find a house. No problem, we presumed, as something would come up in that time. Or so we thought. Over the next six weeks I realised how hard it was to get a rental. The few that did come up we did not get, nor could we afford the rental bond. With weeks to go we had nowhere to live. Finally, we found a temporary place 25 minutes away in Rangiora, it was only short term accommodation but it gave us another three weeks to find a place. The owner was an incredible Christian lady who wanted to rent the place only for short term periods so she could help people who had become homeless from the Christchurch earthquake. We were so thankful for her decision at this time as short term rentals were a rarity.

We believed God had a spot in Oxford for us, but right now we had to take anything. We were so grateful for that spot. We always remember it because when we got to the house in Rangiora the red light for the petrol came on. We had only enough money left for a packet of nappies and a few basic food items. We spent the weekend at the house until money came through on the following Tuesday, allowing us to go back to Oxford. God had got us there but only just.

After three weeks in that house, an Elijah and the widow type of situation arose for us. God used this example in scripture to help encourage me that I was walking in faith. In the biblical story, Elijah is provided for by a poor widow. "*Go at once to Zarephath in the region of Sidon and stay there. **I have directed a widow there to supply you with food**" (1 Kings 17:9).*

In our story an elderly lady who worked at our son's daycare in Oxford said to me, "If you need a house let me know and I will move into my daughter's house for a little while and you can live in mine." I don't know many people who would make such an extraordinary offer of giving up their own house for a time to help someone else. To be honest, normally I would never have even considered a proposal like this, but when I got home and prayed, the ladies' offer kept coming to my mind. Surely, I could not consider this? Sure enough I felt that I was to ask her if we could have three weeks in her house, enough time to finally find the rental we were needing. She was literally excited about the privilege of helping us out in this way and that was how I knew that this was a 'God thing'. When we moved in I gave her $250, with the intent of paying this each week for the three weeks. She said she did not want the money. Eventually I managed to convince her to take it, but she said that I was not to give her any more money. I did try to give money to her again, yet she was adamant that for her this was also an act of faith, that she wanted to do this as an act of love for God and us. We needed to receive her generosity. Sometimes we can struggle to receive from others and this often comes out of the mentality that 'we are on our own' and 'we need to make it happen all by ourselves'. This is not how God ever designed us to live. We are not orphaned but have brothers and sisters wherever we turn who want to help us out. I have learnt to receive when I know someone is acting in faith and from a motive of pleasing God. I will not get in the way of the blessing God wants to not only give us but to give to them too. We have had the privilege of being the blessers many times in our lives and I know the reward that comes from this. I would only struggle to receive from someone when I sense the motive is wrong. Maybe they are not giving from faith but from guilt or fear or that they feel obliged in some way. When Elijah trusted God in depending on the widow's provision, not only was he blessed with provision but the widow was also blessed and got to see her son come back to life.

CHAPTER 7

When we give or receive in faith we get to be part of God's blessing. Yet over and above this, we get to have the deep satisfaction that we are doing what our Father is doing and this gives him great pleasure. We get to walk in the Father's pleasure and there is nothing quite like that.

So after three weeks in temporary accommodation and now a further three weeks in this lady's miraculous accommodation, we were getting pretty tired of moving about, especially with two kids in tow. This needed to be our last move; God had to come through for us. Whilst living in this lady's home we heard from our good friends, Barry and Judy, that their friends were about to rent out their house. I really wanted to try and cut down costs so I was determined to see if I could chat with them before they went to a rental agency. I knocked on their door and was pleasantly surprised to find out that the man who owned the house was Australian. We quickly found a common interest in the sport of rugby league and connected immediately. The house was a beautiful old two storey structure overlooking green fields with a little paddock adjoined to it. It seemed perfect for us. At the end of our chat I asked if he would rent us his home privately and that I could offer $350 a week. Little did I know that he had just found out that he could get $380 through the real estate agency but about $30 of that would go to the agent, so he was happy to rent it to us. Even better was that he asked for only two weeks rent as a security bond and did not require any rent in advance. A real estate agent would usually ask for a four week security bond and two weeks rent in advance. We did not have anywhere near that amount of money available. So, I paid the security bond and we began to move our things in, with the first week's rent to be paid on the Friday when we officially moved in. At the time, as I have been describing, we lived in faith and had very few regular supporters or payments coming into our account. Every week we needed God to provide some of our income supernaturally for us. On this particular Friday there was only $150 in our account and we had moved all our stuff in. We did not even have enough money to pay rent. Had God let us down? Had he set us up to fail? What a terrible witness to the owners of this house, that this Christian family could not pay their first instalment of rent.

One thing I have learnt is that when God provides, it is sometimes very supernatural and other times it occurs in a very 'normal' kind of way. On this occasion he decided to do it in the latter. As I have said before, I never assumed that any person 'should' help or provide for us, that was God's job and yet God would often use people to do this. I rang my friend and mentor to tell her our predicament. Tonight the rent was due and we couldn't pay it.

"Could you please pray for us?" was my plea. On hearing this she asked how much we needed.

"$200," I replied.

"I won't pray for you James but I will be your answer. I will pay for your rent this week."

An 11th hour answer had come and one that occurred in such a normal kind of way. We never once had to miss rent after this and we always had the money to pay. This was a test of our faith and our ability to believe in the goodness of God. He had come through again. He is the rewarder of our faith **(Hebrews 11:6)**.

God's provision through faith often comes with a message or reveals something about God's character. His provision is so often unique and personal, it could only be from God. Think of Elijah and the ravens, Moses and the Israelites and the manna from heaven, the disciples seeing 5000 people fed with five loaves of bread and two fish. There could be no denying in any of these circumstances that this was an act of God.

When we were working full time with YWAM we did eventually gather regular supporters who gave us weekly or monthly money. To be honest, this was only enough to cover the very basics so we still needed to trust God for many things. Oftentimes we would run out of money prior to our next payment and would have to trust God to look after us until then. One Sunday we had run out of money and our next payment would come in on a Tuesday. The cupboards were bare, even to the point where we had no bread and milk left. I cried out to God for a miracle. I knew I could ask someone for a loan, but my first port of call was always to ask God. After church that day we got home and the kids asked if they could run a stall out the front of the house. They would often run a stall selling books and toys, trying to make a few dollars to buy lollies with. They rarely made much but it was fun and because we lived on the main road of Oxford there were plenty of people passing by. After a little while the kids came running in to say they had made $20. A friend from church had driven past and given them the money as a donation. Little did he know the predicament we were in that day. I said to the kids, "We will go up and buy some ice blocks, but Dad also needs to buy some milk and bread too." They were happy enough with this arrangement. After this I really wanted to tell my friend that he had participated in a miracle that day, so I rang him up. He was happy to be part of this and I thanked him for being God's vessel. He hung up and I thought nothing more of it until he turned up at our door several hours later. He had four or five shopping bags full of groceries for us. Not only that but he had given us some venison meat from a recent hunt containing all kinds of sausages and steaks. We ate like Kings and Queens for the next week. The overwhelming message from God was "I have got your back, just trust me. I will care for you."

Another way that I learnt about faith, and the prophetic message it carries, was when I was travelling back from a YWAM outreach on the North Island. My wife and another couple had flown straight to Christchurch, but I needed to go to Tauranga and drive a trailer back with some possessions that we had stored at a friend's house. I had decided to stay at my friend's house for the night. They were an older couple whose children had grown up and they had the most beautiful house you could imagine, with views of Mount Maunganui and the most delightful gardens. That night I found out that my friend had lost his job. He was very down about it and it had taken a hit on his self-worth and esteem. It was not so much about the money, although I'm sure that was important, but it was more about the effect that this had on him. His confidence in God was low and he was no doubt questioning God's goodness. I decided to pray with him. As I did, a thought came to my mind. I was to empty my wallet and give him whatever money I had in there as an act of faith and a declaration that God was going to provide for him again. All I had in my wallet was $25, but I knew this wasn't about money. Rather, this was a message that God wanted to give to him. When I gave him the money I told him as such, that God was going to provide for him and that he would see his goodness again. He was visually touched by this and I knew something had happened in the spiritual realm. Weeks later he received a wonderful job that gave him a lot of satisfaction and much needed income. I had nothing to do with the job, but God allowed me to encourage him through

CHAPTER 7

that tiny act of faith.

My wife taught me something very important about faith after we got married – if you want something, ask God. Often I would say that we do not have the money for this or that and she would simply say, 'I am asking God for it.' It was a very simple and childlike faith she had and God would answer her. In **Matthew 7:7-8** we are told *"**Ask and it will be given to you**, seek and you will find, knock and the door will be opened to you. **For everyone who asks receives**; the one who seeks finds; and to the one who knocks, the door will be opened."* My wife takes this scripture very simply and when in need asks God. This is not just in big things but in tiny little things that God uses to say 'P.S. I love you'. I can remember going up the hill in Welcome Bay, NZ, near Faith Bible College to visit our friend Yarn one time. He lived in a beautiful spot overlooking green rolling hills. Yarn was a very generous man who had a truly unique and quite amazing relationship with God. He spent hours of his day talking to God and then sharing what he had heard with others. You always walked away encouraged when he spoke with you. On this occasion he said he wanted to give us two hammocks that he had. Carolyn was over the moon with this because she had been asking God for a hammock and even the colour was what she wanted. It was these simple acts that strengthened her faith, sometimes much more than the larger things. When we were living with limited resources she would ask God for things like haircuts. Sometimes this didn't happen straight away, but God would always come through.

She also has a real sense of when to just give things away. When we moved to Australia I thought it might be a good opportunity to sell our possessions and make some money. There is nothing wrong with buying and selling things and, as I said before, we are living under the system of capitalism and God uses this system. However, on this occasion we felt like God was saying to give it away. It was a great joy to drop our car down to a friend's house who really needed a van to ferry the kids around. It was also a great moment to walk our trampoline over to our friends down the road, knowing they would get great memories from it. Carolyn's sister and brother-in-law had given us that trampoline and it was a huge family size, top of the range one that even I could bounce on. With God the blessing flows from one person to another when we learn to walk in faith. We may not make maximum money out of it but we sow into God's Kingdom and allow him to determine what we reap. With God there is always a reaping that comes from our sowing. **Galatians 6:7** says *"Do not be deceived: God cannot be mocked. A man reaps what he sows."* We never lose out with God.

God's provision will often come with a mark that says 'this gift is from your Heavenly Father'. It is his way of saying that you are in the right place at the right time. When we moved to Australia we needed to have a van ready for us when we got there, as well as a trailer. This meant I had to try and purchase it from NZ before we left. This was an act of faith in itself. I looked around at vans for quite some time, but many were too expensive or too small for eight growing bodies. Eventually, I found a Hyundai Imax in our price range which had plenty of room for eight and looked to be in good condition. I rang the lady and made an offer a few hundred dollars short of the asking price. Without any hesitation she said, "You can probably have it for $1000 less than the advertised price." Her only reason for this was that "you sound like a nice person and I have been mucked around before and am happy to let you have it for that price." Who drops the price of something by $1000 when I had already said I was prepared to pay substantially more? This had all the marks of God on it. When we arrived at Sydney airport after a stressful and sleepless night, we did not need any more mucking around in the city. We were tired and wanted to get to our first destination, a four hour drive north. We caught a taxi to the lady's house and the van was ready. She had placed in the vehicle a box of fresh fruit and bottles of cold water and allowed us to store our bags at her house while we picked up the trailer. I will always remember her kindness to us when we felt vulnerable and tired after embarking on this huge adventure. Both the van and trailer ended up being in amazing condition and perfect for us. This was just another sign to remind us that 'you are in the right place'.

As we had to drive from NSW to Queensland, where we would live, I told the previous owner of the van that I would need to drive without changing over registration until we got to Queensland. That way we would only pay for registration in one State. I gave her all my details and said that I promised I would pay any fines that we might receive against her registered vehicle in NSW. She was ok with this. When we got to Queensland a week later we went to get the vehicle registered in our names. The clerk at the desk said, "It is already registered in your name". The previous owner, at her own expense, had registered the vehicle for us. You could be cynical and say that she was worried about getting fines for the vehicle but I think she wanted to be a blessing. This was another little way that the Father said, "Welcome to Queensland."

One thing that is very important in faith is laying down a fleece for God to work through. This is not doubting the word of God but sometimes asking the question 'Is that really you God?' and using a fleece to gain an answer in faith. This comes from the story of

Gideon when he puts down a fleece for God. If the fleece is wet the next morning and the ground dry then this will confirm the word that God has spoken to him. When this is confirmed Gideon asks God for a second fleece. This time he asks that the fleece comes back dry and the ground around covered in dew. God does this for him again and now God's word is confirmed in his heart.

> **Judges 6:36-40**
> *Gideon said to God, "**If you will save Israel by my hand as you have promised— look, I will place a wool fleece on the threshing floor. If there is dew only on the fleece and all the ground is dry, then I will know that you will save Israel by my hand,** as you said." **And that is what happened.** Gideon rose early the next day; he squeezed the fleece and wrung out the dew—a bowlful of water.*
> *Then Gideon said to God, "Do not be angry with me. Let me make just one more request. **Allow me one more test with the fleece,** but **this time make the fleece dry and let the ground be covered with dew." That night God did so.** Only the fleece was dry; all the ground was covered with dew.*

When we finished at YWAM we desperately needed to rest as a family and have a break from the base in Oxford. A friend suggested going to a Family Ministry School, which would involve our whole family. There was one in the North Island of NZ and several running in locations around the world. The NZ one was in the midst of change and did not have a school and daycare on site for the kids. What caught our eye was a Family Ministry School on the other side of the world in Norway. At the time this was a far-fetched idea as we actually had no money to go and had never even dreamed of going to Norway. The idea, however, would not go away and it felt like a God thing. So I put out a fleece. My fleece was that I would begin to apply for the school and actively pursue it, but God needed to provide the first $10 000 of our trip without me asking anybody about it. I was very specific about the $10 000, as to go on this trip we would need a lot of money and I wanted to know if this was God. I put the applications in and waited. There was nothing more that I could do. One evening a friend of ours, who had helped us financially when we were leaders at the YWAM base, rang.

She said, "I hear you are thinking about going to Norway for a school. Well, Laurence and I have been praying about it and we would like to give you $10 000 to help you get there."

I nearly fell off my chair. "Did you say $10 000?" I had not told anyone except Carolyn about my fleece. I got great joy out of explaining my story of the fleece to our friend. This act of generosity gave me faith that God wanted us to go to Norway. We still needed $20 000 to go, but in my heart I was now convinced. Not long after this I went up to the North Island to process my time in YWAM with Ray Totorewa, our NZ leader. As I drove to Mount Maunganui to meet him, I was interrupted by a phone call. It was the treasurer from Oxford church, the church that we attended.

"James I just wanted to tell you that someone has given you an anonymous gift of $15 000."

Wow, just wow. I could not believe what I had just heard and I had to ask him to repeat the amount again just to check I heard him correctly. We had never been given a gift like this through the church before, nothing even close. I was over the moon and enjoyed telling Ray about it. After our meeting I went back to my friend Mark's house and told him the story.

"We now just need $5000 and all our flights and school are paid for," I told him.

After I told him the story he said, "That's funny because we were wanting to give you $5000 for the trip as well."

I could not believe what God had done for us. We were going to the Family Ministry School in Norway!

Norway turned out to be a life changing time for our family. We made great friends and received ministry, counselling and training for our marriage and family. Our kids will always remember Norway; from arriving in knee deep snow on the first day of Spring and being totally unprepared for the cold, to enjoying the sunniest May that they had had in decades. We loved Norway. I got to see moose in the wild as well as badgers and deer. The school was amazing but it all began with that fleece, all those months before.

God is truly a generous God and he wants to be a blessing to us. Sometimes the blockage for him to provide for us is an independent spirit that says "I am on my own. I don't need anyone else. "This is what we might call an orphan spirit and in **John 14:18** Jesus says, *"I will not leave you as orphans, I will come to you."* Satan himself was the first orphan, separated from God's blessing and wanting to do it on his own. Satan makes five 'I will' statements in **Isaiah 14:13-14.** These indicated his desire to be 'like' God and to even be above God. He wanted to be separate from God and do life his way.

CHAPTER 7

> **Isaiah 14:13-14**
> *You said in your heart, **"I will ascend to the heavens; I will raise my throne above the stars of God…***
> *…I will ascend above the tops of the clouds; **I will make myself like the Most High."***

When I speak here of being an orphan, I am really referring to a spiritual orphan, someone who lives like they do not have a Heavenly Father. We may call God 'Father' but we live like he has no interest in our lives. Even as Christians, we can struggle with an orphan spirit. We can have a spirit of independence in us that thinks like an orphan, or a person without comfort. We can think, 'I have to fight for everything, I have to compete against everyone else, even to get a position in ministry. I have to make this happen myself as I am on my own. God won't look after me so I have to look after myself.' These are all lies that drive us to live with an orphan spirit.

The Spirit of an orphan will drive you away from dependence on God and interdependence with others. I often lived like this as a Christian for the first seven years of my Christianity, so I am aware of the damage this attitude can bring. When we have this Spirit we often focus on how much we have to love God and how much we have to do to please him yet find it hard to be loved, accepted and valued by him. This is very much an enemy of faith. We need to have the revelation that we are no longer his slaves but his children. **Galatians 4:7** says, *"You are no longer a slave, but God's child; and since you are his child, God has made you also an heir."* We do not need to work for his favour because we already have it.

I once prayed for a man at church who had grown up with a father who had taught him that in life you have to do everything for yourself. This had now become part of his mantra in life as well. This had affected his relationship with God in a major way as he now no longer thought he could ask God for help or provision. He thought that God wanted him to do everything for himself. This is a major roadblock for faith because Jesus said that we need to change and become like little children. In **Matthew 18:3** Jesus said, *"Truly I tell you, unless you change and become like little children, you will never enter the kingdom of heaven."* Jesus was not asking us to become childish, demanding things and throwing temper tantrums, but to become childlike. One thing children know how to do is ask for help. If you cannot ask for help, you will find it hard to be childlike. The Father is always willing and available for us. He loves to answer us and reassure us. Yes, he can say 'no' to us as I have already said, but if he does, it will be for good reason. Your position of faith is to 'come to him' and just ask. To knock on his door and know that he will answer. **(Matthew 7:7)**

When Carolyn and I first got married I struggled being married to a true introvert. Carolyn was often wanting time on her own. Sometimes even on a Saturday night, a night I always saw as a social night. Sometimes I would come to her and she would say, "Can you please leave me alone as I need time on my own?" For years I dealt with this rejection and couldn't understand it. God said to me one day "Come to me. I am always available for you." This helped me get free of the feeling of rejection. Yes, sometimes Carolyn would be unavailable to me, and that is ok, but God was always available and never too busy or wanting to be left alone.

You are not alone, nor do you need to do it all by yourself. God has given you his spirit of sonship that cries out "Abba Father" **(Galatians 4:6)**, an intimate term meaning quite literally 'Daddy'. His

Spirit is always there with you, communing with the Father. Faith requires that you 'come' to him and believe that he will answer you and provide for you. Our beliefs about God are the starting point for faith and I will talk about this more in the next chapter.

CHAPTER 8
KNOWING THE GOODNESS OF GOD

One of the most important factors of faith is how you really view who God is. It is very hard to believe that God can do something amazing for us when we don't believe that at his very heart, God is good. In many churches the statement 'God is good' is a common expression, but it does not mean that this is a true reflection of the way we see him. I was reading **Psalm 118** a little while back and I could not stop reading **verse 1** – *"Give thanks to the Lord, **for he is good;** his love endures forever."* The statement that **"he is good"** just blew me away. Not just because it was in words in front of me, but because I could honestly say that it was the truth. When we know that God is good we can trust his character, we can begin to expect good things from him, even when life is not easy and there are times that might be tough. I love the story of the paralytic man whose four friends made a hole in the roof and lowered him down to Jesus. They must have known that Jesus was good, to believe that they could do such an audacious thing and that he would respond by healing the man. There was something about Jesus that assured them that he would not turn them away or rebuke them for interrupting the meeting but instead profess his forgiveness of the man and heal his body. This was the goodness of God in action.

CHAPTER 8

Luke 5:18-20

Some men came carrying a paralyzed man on a mat and tried to take him into the house to lay him before Jesus. **When they could not find a way to do this because of the crowd, they went up on the roof and lowered him on his mat through the tiles into the middle of the crowd,** *right in front of Jesus.* **When Jesus saw their faith, he said, "Friend, your sins are forgiven."**

Luke 5:24-25

So he said to the paralyzed man, "I tell you, get up, take your mat and go home." *Immediately he stood up in front of them, took what he had been lying on and went home praising God.*

What is your view of God? Is he a slave driver? A harsh and demanding God? A passive, far off deity? Or is he a loving Father who has your best interests at heart?

Jesus came to reveal what God the Father was really like. The very people who were supposed to know him the most, the Pharisees, couldn't recognise him. Phillip, one of the disciples, said to Jesus that if he could see the Father that would be enough for him. Jesus replied, *"Don't you know me, Philip, even after I have been among you such a long time?* ***Anyone who has seen me has seen the Father.*** *How can you say, 'Show us the Father'?* ***Don't you believe that I am in the Father, and that the Father is in me?" (John 14:9-10).*** Jesus was essentially saying, 'If you have seen what I am like, then you know exactly what my Father is like. We share the same DNA and the love that motivates us comes from exactly the same source. The very things that I say and do, my Father says and does. The things my Father says and does, I say and do.' Sometimes

I think we get caught up on a few isolated scriptures that people paint to describe God in a less-than-loving way. I always point them back to Jesus. What was Jesus like? Everything that Jesus is, is what the Father is like too.

Prior to going to India for my outreach at Faith Bible College, I spent two weeks at home serving in NZ. The first week I spent helping a Pastor friend of mine in Tauranga and the second week I worked on a kids holiday camp. I have never been a good sleeper and for as long as I can remember I have suffered terrible sleep when there are unfamiliar beds, noises, or the presence of others close to me (other than my wife). The first week when I was helping my friend, I slept on his lounge room floor and awoke rather early each morning. At the end of the week I was getting pretty tired. From there I went on a seven day kids holiday camp. When I was there I had to sleep in a cabin with eight ten year olds, snoring, breathing and rustling around on a terrible bunk bed for six nights. During the day there was no assigned time off and I was expected to even spend the free time blocks with the kids. By day four of the camp I was exhausted, tired and just wanted to get out of there. In hindsight, I should have spoken up and asked if I could have gotten some rest, but I didn't really know how to do that then. So an ongoing message developed inside my head that went like this: 'God is a slave driver'. All I could think was that all God wanted out of me was my work. I got through to the end of the camp and it was not a great experience for me. Afterwards I drove down to a beautiful surfing break called Raglan, which is on the west coast of the North Island of NZ. It is not famous for beautiful beaches nor warm water but rocky, cold surf breaks that create finely shaped waves that break with raw power and often result in perfect barrels. On this day the waves were at their absolute best with surfers coming out of perfect barrelling waves. At the time I was a keen surfer and I had brought my surfboard with me. I sat beside the water, watching the waves for a couple of hours with the intention of going out there. Yet all I could think about was how exhausted I was and how God was such a slave driver. God's character, in my mind, was on trial. Thankfully, I had been walking with God for long enough by then to know a Father who could be fun, generous and was interested in rest. He was not a Father who just wanted my work. When I went back to my friends I said I was going to stay at the Youth Hostel for a few nights because I just needed to experience the goodness of God again before I went to India. For the next few days I spent time with God in prayer and in his word, went for runs on the beach and surfed. I started to regain some of my strength and the voice in my head was becoming softer. Then on Sunday evening I went down to the surf at Papamoa, right at dusk. The surf there was always pretty small but it could be fun. I paddled out and pretty much had the place to myself. I hadn't sat there long when a big set of waves came from nowhere. I paddled to get on the wave before it broke, stood up and rode the wave across the face for what seemed like forever. It was most likely less than ten seconds before I came to a stop right on the sand. It was the biggest and best wave, by a long way, that I had ever caught at that beach break. A big smile formed across my face and I let out a yell of delight. In that moment I experienced the goodness of God again and I could move on from the last few weeks. I was ready to go to India and share about a God of goodness and not a slave driver.

You will always portray the God that you really know even if God's word says things to the contrary. If deep down you believe that God is angry, then that is how you will portray him to others. If you believe God is a hard task master then this will become evident to others too. We must constantly be looking for the goodness of God even when situations are not ideal. Many people have found the goodness of God in prison, on death row and even when they are sick in bed. My friend Peter Haynes portrayed the goodness of God to everyone around him even when he was dying of cancer. I will always remember my last conversation with him just weeks before he passed. He was so interested in my life and was still believing that God could heal him. He was in considerable pain and yet was still wanting to leave people feeling good about themselves. That was Pete, but it was also the goodness of God being reflected in him.

I recently watched a documentary about the Bali nine. If you are not familiar with this story, it is about nine young Australians who were caught taking heroin out of Bali and were given the death sentence, even though only two have so far suffered this fate. In the midst of immense stress and with the threat of death over them, Andrew Chan and Myuran Sukumaran, the so-called ringleaders, discovered a relationship with Jesus Christ. Andrew Chan became an ordained Pastor in prison and led many to faith in Christ. His countenance changed and the light of God shone through him. The interviews with him were of a young man who had found the very light and life of God in the darkest of places. He did not want to die, I want to make that clear, but he found a new life and reflected the goodness of God in that prison. Myuran Sukumaran became an artist in the prison and produced amazing abstract art pieces, quite often portraits of people that portrayed a message. In the last 72 hours before Myuran was executed he produced about 20 pieces of art, many of them self-portraits and some with a message against the death penalty. One of the most amazing moments was when Andrew and Myuran were led out to be executed. They, along with six other prisoners, all sang songs of praise together. They started with Amazing Grace and finished with Bless the Lord O My Soul. They faced the firing squad without blindfolds, singing praise to God all the while. They had discovered the goodness of God in their darkest moments.

I haven't mentioned anything on healing in this book so far and what better place to mention this than in the chapter on the goodness of God? When Jesus came out of his time of fasting and temptation in the desert, his first words were *"The time has come. The **kingdom of God has come near**. Repent and believe the good news"* (**Mark 1:15).** He would now begin to show what the Kingdom of God was really like. He went about restoring people back into relationship with the Father and this was his number one mission. However, he also spent considerable time restoring people's bodies back to how they were created to be. The miracles of Jesus are one of the major themes of the New Testament gospels. Jesus loved healing people and to see their lives restored, especially after they had suffered. Think…the lady with blood, the centurion and his servant, many lepers, the paralyzed man, the demon-possessed boy, the blind men, and the thousands of others who had their bodies healed by Jesus. They experienced the goodness of God in such a tangible way.

I believe that the posture of our heart is that Jesus can heal anything. If he doesn't then that is his prerogative, but we keep believing in his ability to do so. Sometimes when things don't happen the way we imagine we can examine our own belief and say "Did I not do enough or believe enough?" This just puts the burden for faith all on us, but as I said in the first chapter, faith is initiated in the Father and we respond to him. With faith we get to do a very small part and God takes the heavy load. Jesus said that our load was as small as a mustard seed and yet could initiate huge things. *"Truly I* tell you, ***if you have faith as small as a mustard seed,*** *you can say to this mountain. 'Move from here to there', and it will move.* **Nothing will be impossible for you**" **(Matthew 17:21).** Jesus tells us that nothing would be impossible and yet this comes from such a tiny seed. With faith God gets all the glory and we just get towed along at the back of the boat.

Believing in the goodness of God sometimes means walking through the delay of faith and still believing in his goodness. When I was in my mid-twenties I developed a back problem. I would be in a lot of pain after exercising and when I awoke the next day I could hardly reach past my knees, even though I could normally go way past my toes. Sport and running for fitness were becoming less enjoyable and more difficult because of the pain. When I went to Faith Bible College we had a quite famous NZ healing evangelist pass through who prayed for my back. He was an old school pentecostal style preacher and he would give you a shove so that you went to the ground when he prayed for you. He had thousands of healing testimonies and was the real deal. Yet nothing changed after he prayed for me and my back was still the same. Over the next few years I got prayed for on a number of other occasions, but still nothing changed. At 30 years old I figured that sport was probably over for me and I developed a theology around this. It went like this: I love sport so the Father must be taking it away from me to ensure that I do not make it an idol in my life.

It was a messed up idea about God, but when things don't happen according to what we expect we will often find a way of explaining it, even if it is not a true reflection of the character of God. I went to a chiropractor a few times but in NZ you could only get a Government subsidy for sports injuries when they occurred as a sudden accident rather than as a chronic overuse injury, so it was expensive. When I first went to the chiro the receptionist asked me to put a date down as to when the injury occurred. By doing this I could get cheap treatment as it would be classified as an accident. I knew that my injury was a long term, chronic one that didn't fall into this category. I told her this but she said just put an approximate date down. At this point I could either lie and get treatment or be honest and pay full price. I decided to be honest, even though I knew I would never be caught. I figured my integrity was still on display before God. I look back now and wonder whether this had any impact on future events. Possibly not… but I wonder.

When I was 34 I still longed for my back to be healed but I also had accepted it and the discomfort. One Sunday, Carolyn and I visited a church whilst we stayed in Nelson with Carolyn's parents. The church was called the Mission Fellowship and they had trained up the whole church to pray for healing and they had many healing testimonies. I wasn't thinking of my back though as I had developed my theology around that. The next day I had also agreed to play in a sports camp with a whole bunch of the local churches, playing all kinds of sport. I knew my back would be sore but I figured I could play a limited amount of the activities and at least participate in a small way. Meanwhile, during the church service a word was given for someone with an injured back to come out for prayer afterwards as God wanted to heal them. Could that be me? Could God actually be calling me out? Even though I had accepted my injury and was at peace with it I decided to go up the front after the service as it really felt like a word of faith for me. A 19 year old girl and her Father prayed for me. It was a simple prayer by two people who weren't even in the leadership team. They said nothing spectacular, nor did I feel anything significant. As I went back and sat down

I just had a sense that I had been healed and I told my wife so. There was no evidence for this, just a sense. The next day the sports camp began and I went at it in basketball, touch rugby, soccer, and volleyball. My back was ok but the worst pain was usually the day after playing. This camp would go for three days and I knew that day two would be the hardest for me. I awoke the next morning and my whole body was sore. I could feel every muscle in my body as this was the most sport I had done in several years. But one thing I noticed… My back was fine. I carried on playing sports for the next two days. I was unfit and sore but had no back pain, whatsoever. I have never experienced back pain since. God had healed me completely. The goodness of God was on display in my life. A word of faith had triggered my belief in God again to heal my back and he had done the rest. What a good God. He had also totally blown up my theology about taking sport away so it would not be an idol. I have enjoyed playing sport in whatever way I can ever since then and it remains a part of the way God has made me. God continues to surprise me with his goodness.

When I joined my first school in NZ, Bethlehem College, I had just come out of bible college and I was passionate about the things of God. I had a word spoken over me that I was to pray for people whenever I had the opportunity to do so. It was at this point I met Lynne. Lynne worked in computer services and although they were part of our staff, they did not join us for devotions and staff meetings and were separate in many ways. I would often head to computer services because computers have never been my strong suit and I would often be crying out for help. On one occasion whilst getting help, she told me she had a problem with the arch in her foot and that she would have to have an operation that was going to cost $32 000. I was really burdened by what Lynne said

CHAPTER 8

and I decided to go and see the Principal to see if there was anything we could do about it. Like any good leader, the Principal listened with compassion but essentially gave the problem back to me and said if I had any further ideas to let him know. At this point I was thinking about how we could raise some money for her operation. After I prayed about it I felt God asked me to invite Lynne to our staff devotions and pray for her as a whole staff. Who am I, God? Why me? I am new on staff and I'm still a pretty new Christian. That was my thought process at this stage.

However, God had his way and I invited Lynne to come. As a staff we prayed for her and she was anointed with oil. I said a very simple prayer and didn't feel anything special. Lynne later wrote, "Monday night I could walk in a normal and painfree fashion without shoes for the first time in months. Tuesday afternoon I could run down steps. I usually step gingerly side on when I go down steps." She also went on to say that she had been fast-tracked into surgery (if needed) and this would now cost nothing. She said, "If that isn't the healing power of God, I don't know what is."

I don't know if she ever got surgery, but Lynne had been healed from pain in her heels. My prayer was not fancy or super spiritual. I believed that God could heal Lynne and he did the rest. My faith was as small as a mustard seed, but God is the initiator and main player in faith. We just hang on at the back of the boat being pulled along. All we do is step out and believe and let him do the rest. We believe in the goodness of God as our starting point to faith but he does the heavy lifting.

A few years later at school I again prayed for a staff member who had a liver condition that had caused him severe abdominal pain and even a visit to hospital. After three months like this he was still in pain and he had lost 11 kilograms. I prayed for Peter and he was completely healed almost immediately. Again, I had said nothing super spiritual and it certainly wasn't because of anything I had done. It was all a gift from the Father and we got to enjoy the ride of faith with him. We believe with the mustard seed of faith we have and God grows a garden. Not long after this another staff member, hearing that God had healed Peter, wanted me to pray for them for healing. If I am honest I wanted to run. Part of that might have been immaturity but another part of me didn't want to be seen as the healer.

We are instructed in **Romans 12:2** to renew our minds. We are told that we are *"transformed* [totally changed] *by the renewing of our mind."* When we renew our minds and allow ourselves to be changed, we can now see the **good, pleasing and perfect will** of our Father.

> **Romans 12:2**
> *Do not conform to the pattern of this world, but **be transformed by the renewing of your mind. Then** you will be able to **test and approve what God's will is—his good, pleasing and perfect will.***

In other words, at times our view of God and his will is blocked or obscured because of the thoughts that we have allowed to enter into our minds and hearts. I shared earlier how my experience on a kids camp meant that I began to see God as a slave driver. It was only when I had my mindset changed that I could see that the will of God was good, pleasing and perfect again. In the world we live in it is easy to get cynical, worn out and overwhelmed. When we get into this place and life does not seem to be slowing down for us, we can develop the wrong view of God and his will for us. The goodness of God can get drowned in the rushing waters of life. This year I decided to take a morning off a week so that I could spend some quality time with God doing something that I enjoy; reading, writing, exercising and swimming at the beach. The joy I get from this time each week is unspeakable and so often I really need it. Exhaustion and discouragement are always lying close to my door. Where I get most refreshed is with God and in his word and out in nature. To be a person who walks in faith, we must first find rest and refreshment. I once suggested to a Pastor friend of mine who was very tired that she take a break. Her response was, "I can't do that because I have to manage everyone else's problems." That is not how God wants us to live.

Sometimes it is really hard to find rest. We have six children and I am a school teacher. We do not have relatives who live near us or anyone who can watch our kids. So it is very hard for us to get a break. But we have to find ways to do this or our thoughts of God get diluted and discouraged. The goodness of God includes the rest of God. Often when there is no way of getting a physical break or holiday, I remind myself of God's promise in **Matthew 11:28** that says, *"Come to me, all you who are weary and burdened, and I will give you rest."* I remind God of his word and that he has promised rest when I come to him. This is not conditional on whether it is the holidays or not. Sometimes, days later I find myself almost complaining that things at work are so calm and I find myself with an easy load. I am reminded that was what God promised to me and I am walking in it. God will give us rest when we are weary and when we ask. It may not be a holiday, but it will be a rest from problems and burdens. As he says in **verse 30 of Matthew 11,** *"My yoke is easy and my burden is light."*

If you are in ministry you are a candidate for losing sight of the goodness of God, drowned by business, responsibilities and maybe even struggling to release others into your load. I have been there. When I was in ministry we spent every day doing something spiritual – praying, evangelism, worshipping, listening to a preacher or preaching myself. People would expect that due to this we must be the most spiritual people, because while they are working we get to do spiritual things. Whilst I will say it was an immense privilege to get to do these things everyday and as part of my job, it was not always refreshing. For me, I am refreshed when I get into nature, to be by myself with God. I love reading the word and journaling scriptures and thoughts. Then I love to go exercise or hike, swim in a beautiful place. Often God will speak to me during this time. When I was in ministry I did not do this often enough. We have a responsibility to take care of our hearts. What do our hearts need? What brings you alive and helps you see God clearly again? Ministry can be so busy that it can bury you. I would check my emails night and day when I was a ministry leader. I became driven into busy ministry but often forgot about my heart. We have to find our rest in God, make room in our hearts for him and know when we need to escape the crowd and climb up a mountain, like Jesus did.

I have had a burnout so I know the damage that constant business and stress can do to you. Often when you mention burnout people relate it to a time of being tired and exhausted. When you are tired and exhausted a holiday or a rest is all that you might need to feel good again. When you experience burnout it can take months and even years to recover. My burnout was only minor and I was not bedridden or unable to take care of my children, but I was disillusioned by life and ministry. My normal ability to fight stress with a 'fight' or 'flight' reaction was virtually gone and there were days that simple things like writing emails or putting laundry away were difficult. I was frustrated and angry with my family and spent 15 months out of full time work just recovering my strength and motivation again. I am still always not far from burnout and have to make sure I pull back when I need to.

I don't believe God ever intended life and ministry to be exhausting and for us to be completely drained of life. Yes, we have days and seasons that are very draining but we also need to have seasons of rest. When we don't believe in a God of rest or a God of comfort then it is hard for us to believe that he is interested in these things for us. I love the scripture from **2 Corinthians 1:3-4** that says, *"Praise be to the God and Father of our Lord Jesus Christ,* **the Father of compassion and the God of all comfort,** *who* **comforts us in all our troubles,** *so that we can* **comfort those in any trouble with the comfort we ourselves receive from God."** God has compassion towards us and knows we are really just like little children in adult bodies. We need comfort, we need encouragement, we need help, we need rest and we need someone to say 'don't do that it is not going to help you'. When you have learned to be comforted by God then you are able to comfort others. Comfort is more than just an idea but a substance that we receive into our hearts that we can then share with others. Scripture says that *"we love because he first loved us"* **(1 John 4:19)**. In other words we can only love when we have received love. We sometimes expect people to 'just love others' or 'turn their love on'. This makes love simply a concept or intellectual idea or act of the will. It is as if you can simply love by trying hard to do it. But that is like telling an orphaned child who has come out of a life of trauma to 'just love others'. Until they begin to receive love themselves, then they are not able to love. We are no different, we need to be loved continuously and receive the substance of love into our hearts before we can love others. Otherwise, it is simply an act of our will that we think we just need to try harder to do.

I have found many people, even very talented speakers, men and women of God, who find it hard to receive love. They might see it as selfishness or something that only a child or very broken person may need. Without learning to receive God's love and making this a focus of our life, we will simply be trying to love out of our own will. We all need to come like little children and receive God's love. I can still remember when I was at Faith Bible College and I was coming out of a very trying season. We had a worship and ministry time and I went up for ministry. I still remember Sammy, who was leading worship, saying, "You may not have heard someone say I love you for a long time, but I want to say that I love you." Then he gave me a big hug. I broke down like a small child and wept in his arms. In that moment I needed the Father's Love expressed through a hug from another human. It was like a transaction of love from him to me, with God the source of this love. It wasn't human love that I was needing but God's love through a human.

What does comfort and love have to do with faith? I would say everything. When we are not loved and comforted, we are always trying hard to do something to impress God and others. We try to initiate faith ourselves. When we have been stilled like David was, we are able to move in faith from a foundation of love and peace. In **Psalm 131:2** David says, *"Surely I have calmed and quieted my soul, like a weaned child with his mother; Like a weaned child is my soul within me."* David had learnt to be comforted and loved by the Father in a way that a child is comforted by their mother's breast. What a picture of comfort that is. I remember each of my six children getting very distressed when they were babies and crying loudly. Mum always knew exactly what to do. She would pick them up and place them on her breast. After breast feeding for a short time they were now fast asleep still attached to their mum. What a picture of rest and dependence this is. It is very interesting that David chose to use this example to show how he had been comforted by God the Father.

When we live from willpower and intellectual ideas we really have no comfort to offer others. We need to let faith come from a spring of love and comfort. When we do that we can keep in step with and move in God's spirit of love.

FINAL THOUGHTS

There are thousands of books you could fill on the subject of faith. There is much I don't have authority on and that is a mystery to me about faith. God leaves enough mystery for us to never quite have him all worked out.

Our modern world tries to suppress faith by suggesting that without absolute evidence, something can't be true or exist. Evidence is important in many situations. Yet, "***faith is the evidence of things not seen*** **(Hebrews 11:6),** so to walk in faith you will have to see things before there is any evidence of it happening. Faith requires us to see things as God sees, before their fulfilment.

Faith requires a different set of lenses from the knowledge of 'good and evil', in which we decide and evaluate what is best according to the evidence available. Faith requires us to see what God is seeing and stand on that truth until it becomes reality. Without faith David would not have become King, Abraham would not have set off with no destination in mind to receive his inheritance. The friends of the leper would not have lowered him through the roof believing that today he would walk. And you and I would not have held onto God's promises through hard times when the evidence was against any kind of positive outcome. Faith goes against the grain of our world and yet it is the economy of God here on earth. Without it we can not please God and we can not see God at work. To have faith is to believe in the goodness of God despite the circumstances of life telling us that, 'it can't happen'.

Faith is our connection with God whilst we live in this world.

The time will come when we no longer need faith or need to hold onto God's word because we will be living with him. Until we see him in the flesh, may we look past the challenges and distractions of life and *"set our face like flint"* (**Isaiah 50:7**). As Jesus said to us in **Matthew 28:20,** *"I am with you always, even to the end of the age."*

Amen.

www.ingramcontent.com/pod-product-compliance
Lightning Source LLC
Chambersburg PA
CBHW040742020526
44107CB00084B/2843